Roger Riordan, Tozo Takayanagi

Sunrise Stories

A Glance at the Literature of Japan

Roger Riordan, Tozo Takayanagi

Sunrise Stories
A Glance at the Literature of Japan

ISBN/EAN: 9783744750783

Printed in Europe, USA, Canada, Australia, Japan

Cover: Foto ©Thomas Meinert / pixelio.de

More available books at **www.hansebooks.com**

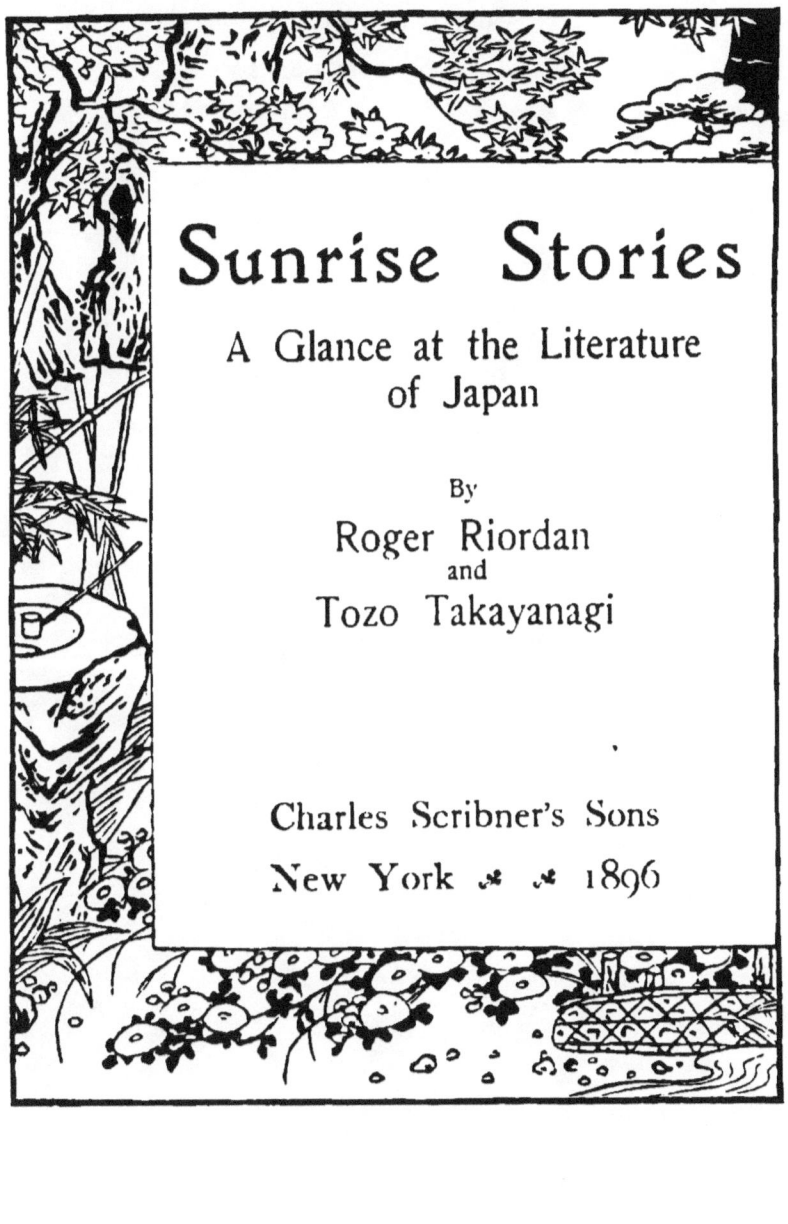

Sunrise Stories

A Glance at the Literature of Japan

By

Roger Riordan
and
Tozo Takayanagi

Charles Scribner's Sons

New York ✼ ✼ 1896

DEDICATED TO

HIS EXCELLENCY S. KURINO

His Imperial Japanese Majesty's Envoy Extraordinary
and Minister Plenipotentiary to the
United States of America
by the Authors

Preface

WHAT is best in the literature of Japan does not bear translation. It is a literature of form without much substance, and, when pressed into the mould of a foreign language, its peculiar beauties are apt to disappear like the opal tints from a squeezed jelly-fish. Handled as carefully as may be, the results are much more likely to excite curiosity than to gratify it, and to send the reader back to those ballads in blue porcelain, those sonnets in chased silver, those poems in old gold lacquer that first drew the attention of westerners to the Land of the Sunrise. Art, whose words are things, whose symbols types, whose grammar beauty, is the universal language that needs no interpreter.

But even the slightest acquaintance with the literature of Japan is likely to add much to one's enjoyment of her art. One cannot miss at least learning something of its subjects, its moods, its history, its relations with the life out of which it has sprung. And a sort of perfume of refinement clings to every idea that has once been given form in classical Japan-

Preface

ese. Nor are more important interests entirely wanting. Historical facts, though not so stubborn as most other facts, and though included here because they are the basis of many fictions, cannot properly be made light of. Myths are now a department of science; the religions of the Far East are no longer spoken of as merely foolish and degrading superstitions; and the songs of Nara, the romances of old Yedo, add to our knowledge of, and pleasure in, humanity.

Still, the reader must not expect to find here much solid instruction. The true inwardness of Shintô, the nature of Nirvana, the import of the irruption of Japan into the charmed circle of Aryan interests, such problems as these must be left to others better able to cope with them. We have to deal more with fancy than with fact, with the brilliant and amusing surface, all foam and glitter, rather than with what may lie below, whether weeds or pearls.

M. de Rosny's " Cours de Langue Japonaise " is, so far as we are aware, the only work in any European language that aims to give a general view of Japanese literature; but it is intended for students of Japanese, and, even in France, is read by few others. It is arranged with little regard to historical development. Within our limited field we have tried to follow the course of past events and to illustrate the history of Japan from its literature, and the literature from

Preface

the circumstances of the times in which it was produced.

Without including the present, four great periods may be distinguished in the history of the country, each of which has had its special literary expression. The first period may be said to have ended at the beginning of the eighth century A.D., when the wandering court of the Empress Jito was fixed at Nara. The second, the period of the early civilization of Nara and Kioto, lasted until the end of the twelfth century. From the thirteenth to the seventeenth century was the period of the civil wars, closed by the battle of Sekigahara, in 1600. Lastly, the period of the Tokugawa Shogunate may be considered to have begun at that date, and to have ended at the restoration of the Mikado's government in 1867.

The Japanese possess an uncommonly interesting account of their early legends and beliefs in the "Kojiki," or "Book of Old Traditions," which was reduced to writing at Nara in 712. There is an excellent translation by Professor Basil Hall Chamberlain, which, however, has as yet been published only as a supplement to Vol. X. of the "Transactions of the Asiatic Society of Japan." The "Nihongi," or "Book of Chronicles of Japan," though written only a few years later and dealing mainly with the same traditions, already shows the influence of ad-

Preface

vancing civilization in the softening or omission of barbaric traits given without reserve in the older work. Of this a French translation, by M. de Rosny, has been published, together with the original text, in two volumes. A translation into English by Mr. Aston is promised.

The compilation of these two books of traditions was followed by that of the most celebrated collections of Japanese lyric poetry, by the study of the Buddhist scriptures and the Chinese classics, and, from the ninth century, by an abundant prose literature. Unhappily, there are few translations from which European or American readers can gain even a slight idea of this literature. The best we owe to the scholars already named. Mr. Chamberlain's "Classical Poetry of the Japanese," M. de Rosny's "Anthologie Japonaise," Mr. Suyematsu Kenchio's partial translation of the " Genji Monogatari " (Romance of Genji), Lieutenant Dickens's of the "Taketori Monogatari," and Dr. August Pfizmaier's of the "Isé Monogatari " are the only works worthy the attention of the general reader.

The succeeding period, marked by the adoption of many Chinese words into the language, by the rise of a new Buddhist literature, largely didactic and controversial, and by many attempts to apply Chinese ethics to Japanese social needs, is yet more poorly

Preface

represented in translation. But the popular literature of the Tokugawa *régime* has fared somewhat better. A few novels, not all of the first class, have been translated into various European languages by Dr. Pfizmaier, F. Turretini, Mr. Greey, Mr. Dickens, and others. The remarkable histories and biographies written during this period have been often drawn upon by European writers, and some notion of the work of the great Shintô apologist, Motoöri, may be derived from Mr. Ernest Satow's interesting essay on the "Revival of Pure Shintô." * Since the Restoration Japan has been too much occupied with necessary reforms to produce much original literary work.

We have made use not only of the books and articles just mentioned, but of others, for which due credit is given elsewhere. But we have constantly endeavored to bring out the spirit of the originals, to the extent in many cases of making entirely new versions, and we have avoided making drafts upon books with which the general reader may be supposed to be familiar.

Our thanks are due to Mr. H. Shugio, Mr. L. Wertheimber, and Mr. Van Weström for valuable assistance and advice.

* Transactions of the Asiatic Society of Japan, Vol. III.

Contents

xi

Contents

Sunrise Stories

Sunrise Stories

I

THE DANCE—INTRODUCTORY

THE Japanese, if no other people, have danced their way into literature and art. The ancient dance masks preserved at Nara, beautifully carved and painted and inlaid, as are at this day those of Pacific tribes barbarous in all things else, represent the beginnings of painting and sculpture; and the oldest poetry of the race seems to have been that of motion. "When words, and sighs, and exclamations fail to show forth the depth and strength of our emotions," says Confucius, "we break out at last, and all at once, in music, poetry, and dancing." And dancing was the principal means of expression. The chanted words and dress in character only explained the meaning of the dance.

A less cheerful origin for the plastic arts has been suggested in the ancient manufacture of images to take the place of the human victims which in primitive Japan were buried alive about the graves of their lords, until the Emperor Suinin (B.C. 29) put an end to this barbarous custom. Numerous stone and terracotta figures have been recovered of much earlier date than the oldest masks at Nara; but, as the masks are of wood, it is easy to account for the fact that none more ancient than the seventh century remain, and there is no question that some of the dances in which they were used are older by many centuries than the date of Suinin's merciful edict.

Song was the natural accompaniment of the dance; but, when it was thought worthy of being handed down to posterity, it was usually necessary to recount in plain prose the exciting occurrence that had given rise to it. Hence the prose narrative, which, in Japan, long preserved its original form of a running commentary on the songs embedded in it. In reading many of the chapters of the "Kojiki," the ballad poetry of Nara, the "Isé Monogatari," one constantly finds that the story is about a song, that the song was made to dance to, that the dance was the first, unpremeditated expression in art of the feeling awakened by some unwonted occurrence. The entire literature of Japan teems with allusions to the legend which is the subject of the next chapter— the legend of the dance that celebrated the yearly

The Dance—Introductory

return of the sun. From other dances have been evolved the lyric dramas of the Middle Ages. And, even in recent works, the reader is frequently reminded, not so much of ordinary human actions, as of those actions intensified and reduced to rule by the actor's art, which is but a form of dancing.

The Miko, the "darling of the gods," still at this day performs the sacred mirror dance before many a village shrine; half a thousand dancers may still be seen circling with waving arms in the dance of Thanksgiving under the harvest moon; and, on the festival of the dead, white-robed girls, issuing from the cemetery, perform the dance of the Ghosts. At the temple of the Green Lotus, in Kioto, Mr. John La Farge witnessed the Butterfly dance, welcoming the summer, and the pilgrim bands dance the Ondo by the roadside, every spring, on their way to the shrine of the sun-goddess in Isé. But many of the ancient dances are falling into disfavor; many are quite forgotten, like the Genroku Odori, danced about that symbol of royalty, the umbrella, and the dance to the creators, Izanami and Izanagi, on the double summit of Mount Tsukuba, which Mushimaro, in the eighth century, celebrated in the following ode as a quaint survival of old-time communism:

THE DANCE OF TSUKUBA.

On the crest of Tsukuba
   Eagles build their eyries ;
On the crest of Tsukuba
   Pilgrims dance in couples.
" Here is neither yours nor mine,"
   Thus they sing in chorus,
" But the gods dispose of all
   In any way that suits them.
I'm decreed to win your maid,
   You to woo my mistress ;
And, surely aught that is, is right,
   Here, on the sill of heaven."

THE MYTH OF THE MIRROR

In some of the more out-of-the-way parts of Europe where the sun still dances on Easter morning, in honor of the Resurrection, children are awakened early to see it glide across the floor of their chamber, skip from wall to wall, and leap from skirting-board to ceiling. The miracle is wrought with a piece of looking-glass, by means of which a ray is thrown through the window. Though, now, a Christian signification is given to it, the custom is doubtless much older than Christianity; for our pagan ancestors were wont to celebrate the return of the sun with dancing; and, reflected from bits of shell or polished metal, they made the sun dance with them.

Such was, most likely, the origin of Uzumé's dance, the story told to account for which is one of the most transparent of sun myths. There are passages in the Japanese, as in other mythologies, which might be cited in support of the theory of Mr. Andrew Lang and Bishop Eusebius of Cæsarea, that myths are " inventions of wild and bestial folk ; "

but there are also imaginings as graceful as the poetic fancies of the Greeks, and of these is the Story of the Mirror.

The earliest gods (so the old traditions say), who had sprung up like reeds out of the shallow water when heaven was separated from earth, had "hidden away their bodies" and died, or become extramundane spirits, when there appeared a divine couple whose mission it was to create the habitable world.* Standing upon the "Floating Bridge of Heaven" (the rainbow), Izanami brought up from the bottom of the sea, with his coral-pointed spear, the materials with which he formed the first dry land. Descending with his consort, Izanagi, they set out, right and left, to make the tour of the island ; and when they met, the goddess, speaking first, cried, "How delightful it is to encounter a beauteous male!" But at this Izanami took offence, for he thought it unbecoming that the female should be the first to speak. So they made the circuit of the isle a second time, and, when they met again, Iza-

* The only one to be regretted of these vanished deities is the microscopic Sukuna-bikona-no-mikoto, the lord of scarecrows. In his anxiety to see how the first rice ears were ripening, this little divinity climbed one of the stalks. But a passing breeze bent it for an instant, and, straightening up again, it shot him off into unknown space. Still, he is supposed to take an interest in the growing grain, and in some occult way to protect it.

nami said, "How pleasant it is to meet a lovely woman!"

The precedence of the male thus happily established, and an example set for the future race of men, the divine pair set about to create other islands, and gods to people them.

After this Izanagi died, and her husband followed her to Hades ; but, dismayed by the horrors of the place, was obliged to return without her. While making his ablutions at a stream on the island of Awaji, gods were born from each article of his clothing, and from each part of his body. Among them, the sun-goddess, "The Shining in Heaven," and the moon-god, "The August Possessor of the Night," were born of his eyes, and from the breath of his nostrils was produced the "Impetuous Male Divinity," to whom was given the rule over wind, and cloud, and sea. In the myths as they have reached us, this impetuous Susanoö is confounded with the moon-god, and has become quite a complex personality, fond of darkness and storms, violent and ungovernable, but not without some redeeming traits in his character. Disliking the manner of the production of the wild fruits and game which the earth-goddess set before him, he slew her, whereupon, from her wounded body, sprang rice, and barley, and cattle, and the mulberry-tree. For desiring to visit the under-world of abominations he was expelled from the creator's presence. Then, in his rôle as god of storm-cloud and eclipse, he quarrelled with the sun-goddess, Amaterasu, and frightened her by throwing the skin of a piebald horse over the bright loom at which she sat weaving. For this last misdeed he was banished to Izumo, where we shall find him later in more becoming employment.

But, meanwhile, his pranks had so alarmed Ama-terasu that she fled for refuge to a great cavern in the mountains, and, shutting the door of rock upon herself, left the world in darkness. Straightway space was filled with the buzzing of wicked gods plan-ning mischief; and the better-disposed children of Iza-nami, assembled in the dry, sandy bed of the Stream of Heaven (the Milky Way), consulted together as to how best they might induce the goddess to return.

In a similar quandary, when it was a question how to bring Hephaistos back to heaven, the Greek gods, it may be remembered, first tried force of arms, and then the power of wine. But the gods of Japan were dealing with a woman, and the plan they hit upon was adapted to the case. They planted hemp and paper mulberry, and made from their fibres and bark beautiful inner and outer garments for the goddess. They polished gems, and pierced them for necklaces and ear-rings. In brief, all the arts of adornment

The Myth of the Mirror

were invented on this occasion. So, it appears, was the art of architecture, for the carpenter-god raised a splendid palace for Amaterasu. But last, and most important of all, the heavenly blacksmith, Amatsumori, hammered out from meteoric iron a large and shining mirror. Neither heaven nor earth had seen the like.

So provided, they had recourse to divination, burning the shin-bone of a deer in a fire of cherry wood. Needless to say, the bone cracked in the luckiest manner possible, and, confident of success, the assembled deities set out for Amaterasu's cavern. Plucking up a tree by the roots, they hung upon its branches the mirror, the jewels, and the coarse and fine raiment. Then the god Strong-arms was posted close to the rock-door. The other gods, ranged round about, started a glorious bonfire and struck up a pleasing melody. The first harp, of six bows placed side by side with their strings uppermost, and the first flute, of bamboo, were sounded, and, to the music of these primitive instruments the merry goddess, Uzumé, springing on to a hollow platform which resounded under her feet, began the sacred mirror dance.

As she danced she improvised an august song, each word of which is a numeral, as in certain counting-verses repeated by children in their games.

9

But the words have also another meaning which may
be translated thus :

> The rift behold, ye gods,
> Where, to your delight,
> Shall majesty appear ;
> So excellent my charms.

It happened, moreover, that, as Uzumé danced,
her dress, instead of the rock-door, came open, giving still another meaning to the song ; so that the
eight hundred thousand gods laughed mightily, till
heaven and earth rang with their laughter.

Their tremendous merriment excited the curiosity
of Amaterasu. Cautiously opening the door a little,
she asked why Uzumé danced, and why the gods
rejoiced in such unseemly fashion, when, owing to
her retirement, the high plain of heaven and reed-
growing Japan were plunged in darkness. Uzumé
answered that it was because they had found an honorable divinity more glorious than herself. At the
word she held up the mirror, and the Shining One,
looking in it, was dazzled by the reflection of her
own brightness. Astonished, she stepped forth from
the cavern. Strong-arms immediately improved the
opportunity, and drew her forward ; and, then, a
straw rope was quickly passed behind her, and the
gods made it taboo, saying " You must not go back

The Myth of the Mirror

behind this ! " They then led her to her palace ; and from that time to this, the Sun has never stayed in the great cave of winter, but, when she sees the straw rope, turns back betimes to give light to reed-growing Japan, and all the world besides.

III

THE CHILDREN OF THE SUN

THE people who thus accounted for the invention of the arts by the necessity of pleasing womankind dwelt anciently at the southern extremity of the large island of Kiūshiū, which, itself, is the southernmost of the main group of the Japanese archipelago. They worshipped Amaterasu, not only as a nature Goddess, but in a special way as their ancestress.* For, after she had again begun to shine in heaven, the earth was still given over to violent and evil-minded deities; and her son, Ninigi, born to her by the intervention of her necklace, was made mortal, and was sent down to Japan to found a race which should forever govern that favored country justly. He took with him his mother's famous mirror, as evidence of the godship in the family.

The neighbors with whom his descendants had to

* Rather than think of themselves as other than descendants of the Sun-goddess, modern rationalizing Japanese speak of her as a mortal queen deified after death. They can consistently take this view, as no strict distinction appears to have ever been made in the national belief between nature gods and deified souls.

The Children of the Sun

deal in Kiūshiū could boast of no such glorious origin, but regarded the wild mountain gods, or (anticipating Darwin) bears and other animals, as their first parents. The Sun-folk, therefore, undertook to rule over them; but their right to do so was sometimes contested. Pit-dwellers, bear-worshippers, bird-men, earth-spiders, and gods with tails fought with and were conquered by them. At length they overran all of Kiūshiū, and, taking ship under their first Mikado, the third in descent from Ninigi, they sailed to the nearest shore of the main island.

Before following them on this expedition, it is in order to relate the strange adventures of Prince Fire-Shine and Prince Fire-Subside, the first- and the last-born sons of Ninigi. Fire-Shine was a fisherman; Fire-Subside was a hunter. One day they exchanged implements and occupations, and the hunter was so unfortunate as to break the line that he had received from his brother, and to lose the hook. Fire-Shine refused to be comforted by the promise of a thousand new fish-hooks for the one that had been lost; and his brother was bewailing his unreasonable conduct by the seashore, when there came to him a deity who advised him to seek the Sea-god's palace, built of fish-scales, to climb into a cassia-tree that grew by the well before the gate, and there await what might happen.

So Fire-Subside built him a boat, and sailed away to the "Nether Distant Country" in which the Sea-god dwelt, and, having arrived there, did as he had been instructed. In a little while a princess, coming out to draw water from the well, saw the stranger in the cassia-tree, and offered him a drink from her pitcher. The prince, without drinking, put a gem from his necklace into his mouth and let it fall into the vessel ; and the gift was so well received that he was invited to enter the palace. There, in quick order, the Sea-god made a feast for him, and gave him the princess in marriage.

For three years Fire-Subside was so happy that he never once thought of the unlucky fish-hook, or of his home in distant Kiūshiū. But at the end he heaved a sigh, and the unwonted occurrence threw everybody in that happy land into a state of consternation. His new relations, gathering about him, anxiously inquired the cause of his sadness, and, learning of the lost fish-hook, hastily summoned all the fishes of the ocean. They came, thronging the sea, and, in some manner not related, the hook was found sticking in the Tai's throat, and was restored to the prince, who was permitted to depart for his own country in order to return it to his brother. His wise father-in-law presented him, moreover, with two jewels endowed with properties that he foresaw would be useful. One of them caused the tide to flow, and the other made it to ebb.

Fire-Shine's immoderate anger was not appeased by the return of his hook. He sought to kill his younger brother, who at once produced the flood-tide jewel, and made the sea to flow in upon the would-be assassin. Fire-Shine's light was in imminent danger of being quenched forever; but, on his promising to make amends for his unfraternal conduct, and surrendering his claim to the inheritance, the younger brother drew the ebb-tide jewel from his bosom, and the waters retreated as fast as they had risen. Thus it came to pass in course of time that Fire-Subside succeeded his father, Ninigi, and, after a reign of five hundred years, was himself succeeded by his son, born of the sea-princess; whose son, again, it was that led the tribe on their venturesome expedition.

On the western coast of the main island, over against Korea, dwelt another powerful people, with whom the Children of the Sun were obliged to reckon soon after their landing, near where now stands, deep in the water at high tide, the great torii of Itsukushima. A high range of mountains cuts the land in two; and, owing to this fortunate circumstance, they had time to grow acquainted without much fighting. A pact was arranged by which the over-lordship was assured to the new-comers. In return, they left the original proprietors in peaceful possession of their land, and built a temple at Kitsuki "with stout pillars and high rafters, reaching up to heaven," to their god Okuninushi, the Master of the Great Land.

These western folk had their own tales of the nether distant country, and their own notions of the gods, which are now, because of their not having fought to a finish, inextricably entangled with the myths of the conquerors. The Master of the Great Land is to modern and less reverent worshippers known as Daikoku, or "Big-Bag," and his son, Kotoshironushinokami, is more widely celebrated as Ebisu, god of fishermen and market-places. Both are great favorites with those droll fellows, the artists. They correspond, it will be seen, to the Kiūshiū princes of land and sea, the hunter and the fisherman. Ebisu, like Fire-Shine, is extremely prone to anger. For the smallest matter he is like to raise a storm ; so that the good people of Mionoseki, where is his chief shrine, are anxious that he should spend as much time as possible in sleep ; and for that reason, as their song tells, cocks are not permitted to exist there. The place boasts its eastern exposure, not common on the west coast, its wedded pine-trees, and its lack of poultry as among

The Children of the Sun

Seki is a charming town,
   The morning sun it faces,
It clambers up and tumbles down
   In unexpected places.
And Seki's pines that, four a-row,
(An odd one fell) in couples grow,
Sound drowsily, when zephyrs blow
     Softly, oh ! so softly.

Seki is the sailors' town,
   Its god doth rule the weather ;
And if you would not swamp and drown,
   Bring there nor fowl nor feather.
In Seki's streets no cock may crow ;
The breed was banished long ago ;
So that the god may sleep, you know,
     Softly, oh ! so softly.

Still, the ungrateful god sometimes blows big guns off Mionoseki, and the coast is a terrible one to approach in rough weather.

Myth-hunters also trace some connection between Inari, Lord of Rice and of Foxes (a very popular god in the west country), Daikoku, and the August Spirit of Food, whom Susanoö slew, as is related in the last chapter. But Inari is said to be only a sort of Reineke Fuchs, a clever, rice-stealing fox, first humanized and then deified ; and the conception of the

Deity of the Great Land, with his enormous meal-bag and his pile of rice bales, corresponds more closely to that of the Kiūshiū Earth-goddess. Both are personifications of the earth as provider of food for man and beast; and the entire group of stories may signify simply the conquest of the coast peoples by the more settled agricultural tribes. That the story of Amaterasu and her violent brother was known in the west before the coming of the Sun clans appears from a legend, which bears evident marks of western origin.

Susanoö, it will be remembered, when he was expelled from heaven for his misconduct, retired to this land of Izumo, which was then a wilderness. One day, while rambling in the mountains, he saw floating down the river Hi a pair of chop-sticks; from which he concluded that there must be people living farther up the stream. He traced it, therefore, to its source, where he met an old man and an old woman, with a young girl for the third, and all three of them weeping bitterly. Susanoö, who was not all a bad lot, was much affected, and drew from the old man that he was an earth-god, Ashi-nazuchi by name, and that the old woman was his wife, and the young girl their daughter. They wept because of their eight daughters, she was the last, and now she was about to be taken from them. A huge, eight-headed centipede had come up yearly from the sea and devoured one, and the time was at hand that he should come for the youngest, who was called the Princess Inada. A godly indignation was kindled in Susanoö's breast on hearing this story, and he asked what manner of creature this monstrous centipede might be. "It has only one body," replied the Earth-god; "but it has eight heads, and eight tails, and forests grow upon its back, and it trails its length across eight valleys and eight mountains." Thereupon Susanoö, coming to the point, valiantly asked the old pair for their daughter if he should succeed in delivering them from the monster. When they learned that their champion was the younger brother of the Sun, the princess was at once surrendered to him; and he promptly put her out of harm's way and prevented her being a hindrance to him in his movements by cleverly transforming her into a wooden comb, which he stuck in his top-knot.

With the help of the old couple, Susanoö now brewed a quantity of saké,* distilling it eight times; and with it they filled eight great jars, and set them before a gate in an eightfold fence that they put up about the top of the mountain. They had not waited long before the monster appeared and at once began drinking out of all the eight jars of saké. Soon it

* Rice spirits.

was overcome with the liquor. The eight heads lay down to sleep on this side and on that of the mountain; and Susanoö, striding from head to head, with his sharp sword neatly severed them from the body. All that day, the legend tells, a torrent of blood rolled down the valley of the river Hi. The victor erected a palace for himself and his wife. Eight clouds arose about it, and he composed an ode on the matter, as follows:

> Eight clouds arise,
> The eightfold fence of Izumo;
> They make an eightfold screen
> For the lovers to retire within.

The shrine is maintained to this day at Yayégaki. At Hinomisaki is also a shrine to Susanoö, and a splendid temple to Amaterasu. But the most renowned god of Izumo is the Deity of the Great Land, who still at Kitsuki, once a year, mounts his bronze horse and rides through every street in the city, the inhabitants keeping carefully indoors on pain of being transformed into dogs.* His progress over, he enters the house of the High Pontiff, his descendant, and remains there for the night; while in a solitary place on the seashore another high functionary performs a mysterious rite, the nature of which he must

* See Hearn's Glimpses of Unfamiliar Japan.

not reveal while he lives, even to his successor. The son (for the office is hereditary) is instructed in his duties by his father's ghost.

Leaving their new allies to shape all those pleasant stories as they would, the Children of the Sun once more set sail northward, through the green islands of the Inland Sea. They landed near Osaka, where they encountered yet other tribes so far advanced in civilization as to be able to offer a stubborn resistance. Attributing the check which they received to their having sailed against the sun from their last station, they put to sea, and again approached their landing-place from the east. This time they were unopposed. One of the native gods, in the form of a raven (probably the Sun-god in a new shape, suggested by the evening flight of the birds to their nests), guided them through the mountain passes into the secluded province of Yamato, where, after more fighting and miraculous victories, they established themselves, and made the district the centre of their empire. Professor Chamberlain recognizes three cycles of legends in the "Kojiki," or Book of Old Traditions, those of Yamato, Izumo, and Kiūshiū; but all belong to the same mythological stock; going to show that, at the time of the conquest, the southern half of Japan was occupied by related tribes, which had probably crossed over from Korea. At Kashiwabara, in Yamato, the leader of the Sun-folk, Kan Iware Hiko-no-Mikoto, better known by his canonical name of Jimmu Tenno, ascended the throne as the first Emperor of Japan, February 19, B.C. 660, according to a modern computation from the data given in the chronicles.

Gradually the empire was extended north and east. A temple was founded at Isé to the Sun-goddess. An expedition was sent out which conquered part of Korea. Little by little the elements of a higher civilization were introduced from the mainland and were spread by force or by persuasion among the subject tribes. We read of many rebellions, dynastic quarrels, and local wars in which the wicked aboriginal gods opposed the descendants of Ninigi and mimicked the state and circumstance of the Mikado. But the stories of the " Kojiki " and the "Nihongi" become more commonplace and more credible as we read. There are no more palaces of fish-scales, and fewer miraculous births—no more coming and going by the Floating Bridge of Heaven; and, with the advent of Buddhist missionaries some time in the sixth century of the Christian era, truth may be said to have gained the upper hand of fiction. But, let us hasten to add that in Japan she has never, until our own times, made a tyrannical use of her advantage.

IV

BUDDHISM

FOR a thousand years from the founding of the Empire myths and legends still fill the pages of the "Kojiki" and "Nihongi." By that time the conquerors had settled down among their tributary villages and become a nation. The empire was still being extended by wars against the savages of the north and east, and, for a time, included part of Korea; but a few of the Children of the Sun sufficed to lead the levies that put down rebellions and kept the peace along the frontier. The Court shifted about from place to place in Yamato and the neighboring provinces, as convenience or caprice dictated; but these periodical flittings, indicating ingrained' habits of camp life, offered no satisfactory outlet for the restless spirit which they betrayed. Many felt ill at ease in a life of turbulent idleness and gross or childish pleasures, no longer seasoned by toil and danger. The view of intoxicated maids of honor hopping about like sparrows in the palace-yard no longer appeared to them a picture of unalloyed felicity. The gods of the August Kitchen, God Pot, and Goddess Kettle, though duly invoked and guarded against demonic interference by plentiful sprinklings of consecrated salt and dried peas, could not preserve even the divine Mikado from the saddening effects of an inactive mode of life. A consciousness of evil too profound to be washed away in the river, or to be banished by fumigations, grew upon the people of the Court, and they fell a prey to that melancholy that comes upon communities as well as upon individuals when old ideals are found wanting and the time is ripe for rapid change and development.

To these troubled consciences certain Buddhist monks from Korea brought the remedy that Gautama had proclaimed in India when the Sun-folk were still at the outset of their work of conquest and exploration. The new teachers began by emphatically declaring that ground for discontent is to be found in the very nature of existence. Life, at the best, they said, is change, and change implies imperfection, and consciousness of imperfection, suffering. But life is transitory and unreal. What is real is the One Divine Essence, calm and immovable, existing in sun and earth, conscious in man and beast, aspiring in the saint, enjoying an immortality of bliss in Buddha. But to Buddhahood all creatures may attain, when, in passing through the bitter waters of experience, they have freed themselves from the illusions of sense and the desire of selfish contentment. Gautama had shown the way, through compassion, renunciation, and abstraction. To make the path easier for other creatures is to shorten it for one's self. The virtuous man at each reincarnation advances on the road to perfection, and may attain, while yet mortal, to a contempt of earthly things, which is a foretaste of the divine calm of Nirvana.

The doctrine had been profoundly modified in China and Korea before it had been introduced in Japan. The primitive scheme of society common to the three countries, which proposed as supreme ends peace, prosperity, and good fame, and as means, submission to the wise government of divinely appointed rulers, had almost completely failed in China, partly because authority was weak and unable to bestow the blessings that were expected of it, partly because certain districts were already overpopulated. The Chinese not only looked to Buddhism for spiritual consolation, but tried to draw from it a practical remedy for their temporal evils. The result was to throw the idealistic philosophy of the Hindoos into the background, and to bring forward problems of practical morality. At the same time fantastic legends were incorporated into the lives of the Buddha and his saints; images were substituted for ideas, and the creed was brought down to the level of the common understanding. Nothing in this teaching was inconsistent with what was regarded as essential in the old Shintô * belief of Japan. Along with its elaborate system of morals, it provided powerful motives for well-doing in its doctrines of the brotherhood of creatures and progression toward an end which might be variously conceived, but always in an elevated way. For, if the mass of the people could raise their thoughts no higher than to the legendary golden paradise in the west, that, itself, was a conception far above their ordinary wishes and aspirations. The more active found a new field for their energies in building monasteries and temples, adorning them with statues and other works of art, and in protecting their inmates. The more intellectual found occupation in the study of the sacred books, and in the metaphysical speculations to which it led. With the monks came artificers of all sorts, merchants, and scholars. Chinese polite literature and rationalistic philosophy were introduced, manners grew refined, and the gross beliefs and practices of earlier days were abandoned.

One figure stands out prominently among those concerned in the great change—that of the prince

* Shintô means the Way of the Gods, in contradistinction to the Way of Buddha.

Buddhism

Umayado, or, as he is more commonly called, Shotoku Taishi, Great Doctor of the Divine Law. He was son of the Emperor Yomei, and brother of the Empress Suiko, during the greater part of whose reign he acted as regent. Born of a Buddhist mother, he is represented as having been from childhood pious and fond of learning. A wooden statue preserved at Nara, and which is strikingly like the charming reliefs of children by Luca della Robbia, shows him as an infant with hands clasped in prayer. In his youth, as general of the imperial forces, he quelled the rebellion of the Buddha-hater, Moroye. As regent, he reformed the administration of the empire, establishing governmental departments and sending out provincial rulers clothed with authority over the local chiefs. For the guidance of these functionaries he prepared a short code of laws, or rather precepts, advising them to act as peacemakers between chiefs of adjoining districts and to teach the duty of honoring Buddhism and obeying the Empress; they were to observe politeness in the conduct of official business, and to promote capable officers; bribe-taking, favoritism, and the levying of taxes for private use were forbidden; the winter season was indicated for the carrying out of important public works, so as not to interfere with agriculture; diligence, fidelity, and devotion to the public good were required of all officers.

Sunrise Stories

Shotoku Taishi is venerated as the founder of the monasteries of Koriūji at Kioto, and of Horiūji in the hills near Nara, the Founder's Hall of which last still exists, the oldest of Buddhist monuments in Japan. It may help to establish him in the reader's memory to note the year of his death, which was that of Mahomet's Hegira, A.D. 622.*

The effect of Buddhism on the literature that soon came into existence—the classical literature of Japan —shows itself in a more intimate and trustful commerce with nature, in a greater refinement of taste and sentiment, and in a tendency toward the ideal. Its influence, in truth, was not very profound. For this there were several reasons, chief of which was the persistence of the ancient faith. Shintô stood as a rock in the flood of new beliefs, neither submerged nor swept away, as were, at the same period, the pagan faiths of Western Europe. The new religion simply took possession, on the whole peacefully, of the large territory uncovered by the old. To the Western reader nothing is stranger than the constant outcropping of Shintô sentiments in the writings of professed Buddhists. In so far as regards the peculiar type of patriotism which is the essence of Shintô, the national character was already set when the Buddh-

* A Biography of Shotoku Taishi was written by Taira no Motochika about A.D. 992.

ist monks appeared upon the scene. One or two attempts were indeed made to bring about a complete revolution, but they proved utter failures. Neither the zeal of an empress, nor the long anarchy of the civil wars, could undo the work of the early ages. Loyalty, family pride, religion, and patriotism are all one in the Japanese soul. With people of European stock these sentiments may be said to be naturally connected like the leaves in a bud; with the Japanese the bud has hardened into a thorn, which has always wounded the hand that has meddled with it.

The habit of writing on all important matters in Chinese left the cultivation of the native tongue to the ladies, with whom an affectation of intellectuality seems to have become as much the fashion as it is at the present day. Now, they spoil their eyes reading German text, and have abandoned their prayer-books to study Mr. Herbert Spencer. Then, they learned the Sutras by heart, wrote verses, kept diaries, and criticised paintings. One can forgive these far Eastern *précieuses* their little self-conscious airs and grimaces, for with all their learning they are seldom dull. But they are in part to blame for the slightness of the matter and the all-importance of form in the ancient literature of their country.

The exclusiveness fostered by the new civilization,

which was for a long time confined to court circles, gradually cut off the writers from real life and its variety. There is much of natural feeling and frank utterance in the earliest works; but these were soon superseded by such qualities as might be expected of the uncommon æsthetic endowment of the race, kept within strict bounds as to subject and treatment, and forever driven to take refuge in new subtleties, new refinement by a constant and well-founded dread of *ennui.* Courtliness, ceremoniousness, elegance, distinction are almost always present. Their poetry is vague, dreamy, unsubstantial; a poetry in which everything appears against a background of mist; a poetry of trees in blossom, of falling leaves, lapsing waves; a poetry which to attempt to imitate closely in English were to take Boreas for a flute-player.

But in the plastic arts there was great and sudden development distinctly due to Buddhism. The natural turn of the people for æsthetic pleasures must not be forgotten. A long list might be made of the flowering plants and trees mentioned in the " Kojiki." The mortuary images already spoken of give evidence of a sense of organic beauty usually not to be found except among highly civilized peoples. But it cannot be questioned that the main influence came from China and Korea. The most famous of the early sculptors, painters, and architects were foreigners;

and, indeed, the little direct knowledge that we have of ancient Chinese Buddhist art is confined to specimens preserved in Japanese temples and treasuries. It is usual to refer the rise of that art to the fountainhead of Buddhism, India,* whose influence is, indeed, easily traceable; but it is a mistake to describe it as dominant. There is good reason to believe that before Buddhism had penetrated into China, in the first century of our era, the Chinese had already brought the arts of design to a condition at least as advanced as that which they had attained in ancient Egypt. They had most likely proceeded much further in the realistic painting of animals and plants, and in a graphic style of sketching landscapes and figures in ink. Hindoo art supplied them with higher motives, a more solemn coloring, an enthusiasm which they probably lacked. The styles of Chinese painting that were transferred to Japan comprised not only that of the Buddhist school of illuminations in broad, flat tints, bounded by firmly drawn outlines and set off by gold backgrounds, but also the dexterous free sketching in black line and mass, a result of the constant practice with the brush afforded by Chinese ideographic writing, and a style of miniature painting that soon branched into two schools,

* Some go farther and ascribe the beginnings of Indian art to the Greeks of Alexander's army.

one stiff in form and conventional in color, the other minutely realistic, except as to the avoidance of shadows. In Japan, many other intermediate schools appeared. New subjects were found in the national legends and history. We learn from the romance of Genji how paintings were criticised by the ladies and gentlemen of the court. It was *de rigueur* that the decorative effect of the mounts and accessories should first be passed upon, and, to enhance it, the pictures were brought in by young girls whose dress repeated the fundamental tones of the Kakemono. The nature of the subject, whether more or less worthy, was next considered; and, these subordinate matters out of the way, the prize was awarded to that painting which was adjudged to render most faithfully the sentiments inspired by natural beauty.

A Buddha by the first great native painter, Kose no Kanaoka, who was a contemporary of the author of Genji, was shown at the Paris Retrospective Exhibition, and was remarked not more for its strange technique, its strong outlines, its slight modelling, its pale flesh tints starting out from intense dark reds of drapery and background of tarnished gold, than for its mysterious charm of expression, its majestic calm, and quiet grace. But the paintings on the wall of the Hondo at Koriūji, praised by La Farge for their placid elegance, quiet refinement of line, and breadth

Buddhism

of religious peace, are from the hand of the Korean, Tori Busshi, to whom are also due the majestic statue of the Healing Buddha, and various other works preserved there. The most celebrated piece of Buddhist painting in Japan, or in the world, is the immense kakemono on which the Chinese artist, Wu-tao-tse, has depicted the eight scenes of the life of Buddha. A central picture of the death of Gautama is surrounded by others of his birth in heaven, his conception, his birth on earth, his retreat among the ascetics, his temptation under the Boddhimanda fig-tree, his preaching at Benares, the aërial flight of his coffin around the walls of the city of Kousinagara, and his reception into Nirvana.

The golden hall at Koriūji was built and decorated when the mosaics of Ravenna were yet new, and Kanaoka painted when Charlemagne was collecting illuminated manuscripts and sitting up of nights to learn his letters. In splendor and in depth of religious feeling the arts of the East and West were on an equality. In power over form, the Buddhist art, with all its shortcomings, was superior.

V

YOUR CHOICE OF MIRACLES

THE change in religious ideas was accompanied by the growth, in court circles, of a somewhat sceptical and ironical spirit; but the masses displayed a healthy appetite for the marvellous, which, indeed, grew with what it fed on. The legendary outcome of a thousand years of Buddhism in India and China, added to their native myths, did not suffice them. In the age of faith that followed the establishment of the new creed, a host of quaint fictions arose, which have been gathered into many volumes of "Moral and Amusing Tales," and brighten the pages of serious biographies and histories.*

It were easy to find parallels among the contemporary Christian legends of Western Europe for most of the Buddhist miracle stories. Pious fancy that joins together what nature has held asunder is the real wonder-worker; and it was as easy for it to

* As, for example: Gukuansho (Buddhist Tales), by Ichin Osho, 1230; Shashe-Kishiu (Moral Stories), by Mujiu, 1279; and the Biographies of Shōtŏku Taishi, Sugawara no Michizane, and Kŏbŏ Daishi.

carry the Hovering Stone down Severn to Glaston-
bury "in the old time of the King Arthuir," as to
cause the convent bell to float like a big bubble when
thrown into the torrent of the Yodogawa. The doe
that came with full udder to St. Giles in his retreat,
"nosing her way through the branches," might pair
with the deer of five colors that regularly attended
the reading of the Buddhist Scriptures, The tale of
St. Benedict making whole the broken dish by prayer,
caps that of St. Kōbō Daishi, who set a leaning
pagoda straight by the same means ; and Pope Greg-
ory's description of Benedict's sojourn in the Forest
of Sublacus might serve for companion-piece to that
which follows, about the mountaineering hermit,
Shōdō Shōnin.

The scene of the latter's retreat is now the most
famous Buddhist show-place in Japan, celebrated all
over the world, indeed, for the gorgeous shrines of
the two great Tokugawa rulers, Iyeyasu and Iyemitsu.
In the early Middle Ages it was an unknown and
inaccessible valley in the heart of a mountainous
wilderness. While in retreat in the caves of Izuru,
the future Abbot of Nikko saw in vision the four
great peaks dominating the hidden valley, and felt
himself irresistibly drawn to them. The whole way
(it was far to the north) lay over unnamed mountain
ridges. Chain succeeded chain, each trending di-

rectly across his path. They reared themselves against him like a succession of enormous ramparts, and as it was mid-winter the passes were deep in snow. Yet the saint did not hesitate, but, following the promptings of the Spirit, he floundered on through the wide, white, silent landscape until he reached a lofty summit from which he could see, still far away, the mountains of his dream. So high they looked, so far, and, in their covering of snow, so pure and unsullied, that he felt himself unworthy to approach nearer. Here, then, he spent three years in fasting and prayer, in face of the object of his desire. The local divinity waited on him and supplied his needs ; for the country gods in those delightful times everywhere became the humble and devoted gillies of the rambling Buddhist saints, and aided them to spy out the land. But, at the end, he still thought himself unworthy, and returned to Izuru.

The spirit of discovery, however, was strong within him, and, after five years given to pious exercises, he renewed his attempt. He had not proceeded far on his second journey when he noticed that, right and left, before and after, four clouds—one black, one blue, one white, one ruddy—were travelling with him. However far he was obliged to deviate from the direct route, they kept their relative positions at the four cardinal points, and so guided him on his way. He passed his stopping-place of eight years before. A little farther on the only path was crossed by a swift torrent; but, again, the local deity came to his assistance and flung across the chasm a bridge of living snakes, which disappeared the moment the saint set foot upon the opposite bank. There he built him a cabin, and once more betook himself to prayer and meditation.

In answer to his prayers the vision returned, and the four gods that guarded the sacred mountains manifested themselves to him as the Black Warrior, the Blue Dragon, the Vermilion Bird, and the White Tiger, and urged him to resume his journey. Their colors corresponded with those of the clouds that had guided him hitherto; and when again these clouds appeared, steadfast upon four great peaks, he knew that he had at last reached the predestined scene of his life's labors. A small lake lay in the hollow between the mountains. High in a cliff on the further bank was the cave of a wind-god, who obligingly surrendered it to the new-comer. Disciples gradually made their way to the hermit and settled in the valley below. Mite-dropping pilgrims followed, and, by degrees, temples and monasteries arose in the wilderness.

Shōdō Shōnin's successor as abbot was Kōbō Daishi, of whose philosophical treatise on the " Teaching

of the Truth " M. de Rosny has published a translation. Kōbō Daishi was of St. Paul's advice—that
there are " divers ministries," and he included the
concoction of pious fictions among them ; but it may
be doubted whether he would approve of all that are
current about himself. He is famous as calligrapher,
and as the inventor of the Japanese style of writing ;
and it is related that once, in a contest of penmanship
with the God of Wisdom, the latter wrote the character for " dragon " upon the river Ujigawa, but forgot to dot it. Then, at his request, Kōbō Daishi supplied the dot, and the character became a living
dragon, and in a great commotion of winds and waters
ascended from the river into the clouds. There are
tales of other Rishis producing waterspouts, horses,
and dragons from their drinking-bowls, but the following little apologue seems intended to carry a
moral, and that moral appears to be that a steadfast
faith is better than skill in controversy.

At Tosa, where Kōbō Daishi passed his novitiate,
it was customary to try the constancy and the courage of the applicant for holy orders by posting him to
keep watch for a night at the monastery gate. The
rocky platform on which the building stood looks out
over the Pacific Ocean ; and, especially at night, the
vague immensities of sea and sky may well have had an
unsettling effect even on minds thoroughly grounded

in the holy Sutras. Shadowy doubts came to torment the novice in the first hours of his vigil. The wind that whispered in the gloomy cryptomeria-trees, the waves dashing upon the rocks far below, seemed to give voice to his uncertainties. The spirits of incredulity and misbelief at length took form as goblins that started out from the recesses of the wood, and as dragons that writhed up from the abyss, and assailed him on all sides with taunts and outrageous propositions. They propounded unanswerable questions, they hedged him in with sophistries, they opened out distracting side-issues, stunned him with blatant assertions; they howled at him, roared at him, threatened him, insulted him. Every weapon in the armory of unbelief was brought to bear. Like Luther, he was rendered desperate; but, unlike Luther, he had no ink-bottle at hand to hurl at his tormentors. In this situation, unable to confute a hundred assailants at once, he could think of no better way of showing his contempt for the rabble than by spitting upon them. At the moment the rays of the evening star shone full into his mouth, and the demons, to whom it appeared that the holy youth expectorated starlight, were filled with a sudden fear that worse might befall them. The miracle, though but a lucky chance, was too much for them, and they gave up the contest and retired to the depths out of which they had come.

There is one notable difference between these
Buddhist stories and the legends of Christian saints
and missionaries. We nowhere read of these latter
making compacts with pagan gods or taking them
into their service, as appears to have been the rule
with the apostles of Buddhism in Japan. Every
Buddhist monastery has, in fact, its barbarian god for
guardian or protector. And Shintô, Taoist, and
Buddhist miracles make room for one another, so to
speak, as did the myths of Kiūshiū, Izumo, and Yamato. There are cases in which the Buddhist serpent
has swallowed the Shintô snakes, but these are
plainly to be seen, alive and wriggling in its belly.
Shôdô Shônin's four clouds are manifestly a Shintô
invention. The "eternal polity" of the Japanese
was, and is, bound up with their primitive concep-
tions, and in accepting Buddhism, they made sure
that the divinely established order of society was not
endangered thereby. The doctrine of transmigration
made it easy for the missionaries to adopt the ancestral gods of Japan as temporary manifestations of the
Buddha. Thus, when the abbot and sculptor, Gyôgi,
was referred to the Sun-goddess at Isé for authority
to erect the colossal statue of Buddha at Nara,
Amaterasu (probably in the shape of her priestess)
appeared to him on the seventh night of his watching to say that she was herself, in reality, Amida

Your Choice of Miracles

Buddha—the Buddha of enlightenment. To this Buddha, therefore, the great bronze statue was dedicated.

A curious consequence of this mingling of beliefs is seen in prayers of devout nuns and priests, that these Protean divinities would deign to manifest themselves in their true form. A certain artist monk, desiring to paint a true likeness of Gautama, earnestly entreated him to reveal himself, and at daybreak saw the great teacher's countenance in the sun's disk as it rose between the two green crests that fronted on his monastery. Since all Buddhas are one, this miracle is plainly confirmatory of the doctrine laid down by Gyōgi. It was in answer to a similar prayer of the Princess Taema that Kuanon * wove the famous mandara † of lotos fibres, miraculously dyed of many hues in the clear water of the convent well, in which appeared the portraits of the divine weaver, and of all the Buddhist saints and deities. Unfortunately but a small scrap of this famous tapestry now exists.

These Buddhist stories, we may say, are white lies, like the efforts of children to put this and that to-

---

* God or Goddess of Mercy. A manifestation of Buddha usually represented as a female, but sometimes as a male.

† A picture of the earthly and celestial spheres, with a Buddhist pantheon.

gether. They never deceived nor were intended to deceive, and they pleased and instructed a people avid of wonders. But pure Shintô miracles had not ceased, and some of them are of another stamp, such as the tale of the clever young woman who demonstrated that her clandestine lover was a god by tying the end of a ball of yarn to his robe, and so tracking him to his shrine. As a rule, the Shintô miracle is less presentable or less picturesque than the Buddhist.

The powers attributed to the artists of the time are hardly less miraculous than those ascribed to the saints, which is the less remarkable as saint and artist were often one and the same. But the old and widespread superstition that regarded the painter as in the fullest sense a creator, is answerable for the stories told of Kanaoka's horses, and of the passing of Wu-tao-tse.

Kanaoka, the greatest painter of the Buddhist school, occasionally amused himself by excursions into a branch of art which permitted freer handling. He chose the painting of horses, a *genre* which in his day was much admired in both China and Japan. Some of his steeds, it appears, were in the habit of leaving the paper on which they were painted to gallop at night about the country. To one was brought home the crime of having destroyed the

Your Choice of Miracles

Mikado's lespediza beds ; and another was convicted of having in his nocturnal gambols trampled down the growing rice in the fields near by. The former was merely tethered by a strong chain to a pillar ; but the angry farmers who detected the latter by the mud upon his hoofs, took revenge for their losses by scratching out his eyes.

Some account has been given in the last chapter of Wu-tao-tse's great painting of the Eight Scenes. He was even more famous as a landscape painter than as a painter of religious subjects. After a brilliant artistic career in Japan, where his only authentic pictures are now preserved, he was recalled to China by the Emperor, for whom he decorated several pavilions with landscapes in the romantic style of the Flowery Kingdom. On a certain painting of a secluded glen between two rocky and wooded mountains, he expended much time and labor, and was unwilling that any one, even the Emperor, should see it while in progress ; a fact that was remarked upon ill-naturedly by several of the courtiers. At last the picture was finished, and his Imperial Majesty was told that he would be admitted. He went with his customary retinue, which included some critics more disposed to display their knowledge than to appreciate a work of genius. These distressing persons began at once to discover defects in the painting. The rocks were out of drawing; the foliage was stiff and labored; the clouds were too sharply defined; the little chalet hidden among the trees should be more conspicuous, they thought, and its architecture of a less commonplace order. The rivulet did not flow; the air did not circulate; in short, every part of the picture was conceived and executed in defiance of all the rules of art and laws of nature. They ended by convincing the Emperor that it was a mediocre affair, unworthy of his inspection, and that the painter had lost his cunning. To all this the latter listened in silence. But, when they had quite finished, and the Emperor was about to depart, Wu-tao-tse, *who had created that particular paradise to be his own eternal abode*, politely bade his Majesty farewell, and, calmly stepping into his landscape, disappeared among the trees. Then the picture faded away like a mirage, and neither it nor the painter has been seen again.

Numberless examples might be brought forward of the miracle *pour rire*. In Japan those objects that we somewhat hastily term "inanimate" do not need to be bewitched. Umbrellas, lanterns, and bowls of rice may be goblins in their own right, as in the interesting family gathering depicted in a novelette by Bakin. But one may also be the victim of demonic abuse, and be needlessly terrified by things

Your Choice of Miracles

really innocent. The story of the emperor Uda and the demon is a favorite subject with artists in lacquer. His Augustness was on his way, one stormy night, to a place which he should not have frequented,* when he was surprised in a narrow passage by a shaggy and misshapen being which rushed at a furious pace upon him, emitting flashes of fire. The Emperor would have fled, but his attendant, Takamochi, promptly knocked the goblin down, who turned out to be a poor old priest, clad in a straw storm-coat, who was running to relight a votive lantern that had been blown out by the gale. It is not said what was done for the priest, but Takamochi, for his bravery, was promoted to an honorable position, and became the ancestor of the famous Taira clan.

The jolly abbot Toba was a famous creator of comic wonders. Come of a fighting stock—the Minamoto, later the chief antagonists of the Taira—he caricatured both warriors and clergy. He is said to be the inventor of the Japanese ghost, that astonishing bogy made up of a wisp of hair, a shroud, and a wraith of mist, that ascends from some neglected grave at dusk to frighten the penitent widower who comes to offer up a prayer long overdue. From him are all rough sketches of comic intent called Toba-ye. M. Gonse publishes a drawing of his in which a

* Gion Street, the Yoshiwara of Kioto.

45

doughty warrior, mounted on a mouse, his face to the tail of his charger, overturns, while in full retreat, two of his pursuers with a prod of his lance. Toba's men and women are only amusing creations of an irresponsible brush, but he is said to have rivalled Kanaoka as a draughtsman of horses. He seems to have found something hugely comic in the play of these beasts when full-fed and at liberty.

Perhaps those Chinese paintings already referred to, and of which we see copies on Ming vases, may have stimulated his fancy. The present Emperor of Japan is the owner of a screen decorated by him with twelve horses of the size of life, spiritedly drawn in India-ink. The virtues of the herb Pantagruelion must assuredly have been known to this good Buddhist abbot, whose harmless humor, like that of the later comic artists of his race, may be truly described as consisting mainly in "*une certaine gaieté d'esprit confit en mépris de choses fortuites.*"

VI

SONGS OF TWO CITIES—NARA

Now " a ruin in the rice-fields," through which still extend its long avenues of ancient chamæcyparis-trees, and across which for twenty miles around the booming of its great bell still resounds at evening, above the croaking of a myriad frogs, Nara grew up about the monasteries founded by Shotoku Taishi. The great temples of Todaiji and Koriūji, splendid with richly colored wall-paintings and images of gilded bronze, situated with their many dependencies on the verge of a cultivable plain surrounded by mountains, determined the Empress Jito to fix her wandering court there. It became the first settled capital in which the conditions of city life definitively replaced those of the camp.

Jito was a remarkable woman, even for old Japan. Daughter of one emperor and consort of another, she assumed the regency after the latter's death, setting aside and causing to be executed as a rebel the prince Ohotsuno, who had been named for regent by her husband. Her son, who was to have succeeded to the throne, died at an early age, and she had herself proclaimed as reigning Empress A.D. 690. Six years later she resigned the throne in favor of her grandson, Mommu; but he also died, and Jito resumed the crown at Nara in 708. From that date until 784, Nara remained the capital of the empire.

There, under Jito, was compiled and published the "Book of Old Traditions," begun by order of her husband, Tenmu. This first step toward the creation of a national literature was followed, in 720, under her daughter and successor, Gensho, by the publication of the Nihongi, or " Chronicles of Japan." But Nara owed its greatest glories to a third imperial consort, who, though she never actually reigned, is known in history as the Empress Glorious *par excellence*. This was the spouse of the Mikado Shomu, who succeeded Gensho in 724.

She it was who filled Japan with monasteries in every province, each with its school and hospital, each with its little band of scribes and artists constantly occupied in copying and ornamenting the Buddhist scriptures, in carving and painting the images of the saints. Her own copy of one of the holy books is still preserved, and is noted for the beauty of its calligraphy and illuminations. It was owing to the enthusiasm inspired by her that the colossal bronze statue of Buddha the Enlightener was set up, dreaming with open eyes above the groves and housetops of the city.

Society at Nara followed a course not altogether in accordance with the teachings of its tutelary divinity. A sumptuous and refined civilization grew up among the population of idle warriors and courtiers, as the chief result of the labors of foreign scholars, artists, and ecclesiastics. Nara became the home of luxurious arts, of emotional poetry and polite learning. Academies were opened for the instruction of the sons of government officials, where, besides the useful sciences of mathematics and medicine, music, astrology, and Chinese philosophy and poetry were taught. And, though unprovided with special schools, the ladies of the Court were often better instructed than the men, and exercised much influence in every walk of life. The richer among them dressed in gorgeous brocades, their furniture was of costly lacquer, they amused themselves with games played on inlaid checker-boards, and carried their illuminated books of prayers in cases ornamented with gold and amber. The poorer prepared themselves the yarn that hung to bleach on the bamboo fence of the door-yard, and wove it into the coarse cloth of which they made their garments. But distinction seems to have been little based on wealth, and the whole of the Yamato nation, as distinguished from the subject tribes, appears to have been accounted noble. The women generally were taught the music of China, Koma, Kudara, Shiragi, and Kora.* They were allowed a great deal of freedom. They had dances in the fields near the city, and concerts in the open air under the cherry-trees. Masquerading in male attire was permitted on certain festivals, even within the precincts of the palace.

Women had their special superstitions. Their husbands and lovers were often away in garrison on the frontier, or on government business in distant provinces, and, when no newer flame had sprung up to console them, they would consult the "Evening Oracle" as to the return of the absent one, and draw hope or resignation from the first chance words heard while promenading at dusk upon the street. Some charitable neighbor, acquainted with the case, would be pretty sure to hint that the wanderer was already on the road, or was only detained by his desire to complete a string of pearls, a present for his lucky inamorata. "Two days at least, seven days at most," would see him home again. But, at the moment, the unfortunate might be lying slain by treacherous

*Kudara, Shiragi, and Kora were petty kingdoms of Korea, and Koma is believed to have been a general appellation for that country.

savages or overwhelmed by an avalanche in some unknown mountain pass.

Unhappily there is abundant evidence, too, that
the ladies sometimes turned to account their oppor-
tunities for flirtation. It is not surprising, therefore,
the capital being such a pleasant place of abode, and
absence from it in more than one way dangerous, that
to be sent to govern an outlying island or province
was looked upon as a misfortune. Ambitious courtiers did not covet missions of the sort, and on the
Buddhist priests and hermits devolved a large share
of the work of extending the civilization which they
had done so much to create. These intrepid men
opened up new routes in the wilderness, penetrated
into regions believed to be guarded by jealous and
vindictive gods, and established their hermitages in
places where the prayer-sticks of the aborigines testi-
fied to their dread of the demons of storm and flood.
Meanwhile, in the intervals of pleasure or of fighting,
the nobles occupied their leisure in putting into verse
the sentiments with which their life of alternate lux-
ury and danger inspired them. The generation that
witnessed the establishment of the capital at Nara
produced much of the best lyric poetry of Japan.

The first and most esteemed of many collections of
verse was made at the instigation of Shomu and his
Empress Glorious. The odes and ballads of the

"Myriad Leaves," like the stories of the "Kojiki" and the "Nihongi," were largely drawn from the traditions of the more important families, which often took the form of pithy sayings in verse, accompanied by tales or legends relating the circumstances of their composition. The collection includes poems centuries older than the date of its publication; but the time was one of enormous productivity in this way, and may well be called the lyric age of Japan. Hitomaro, the prince of Japanese poets, may have been still alive when the collection was undertaken.* He and many of his contemporaries are represented in it. The number includes its editor, Yakamochi, as an example of whose skill in turning a compliment we give his ode addressed to the Empress Jito, one snowy New-Year's morning, during her first reign at Kashiwabara.

A NEW-YEAR'S GREETING.

TO THE EMPRESS. YAKAMOCHI.

Ceaselessly the snow
From cloudy treasuries falls,
  Inexhaustible.
So may all graces on thee
  Descend, this first spring morning.

* He died in 737. The exact date of the Myriad Leaves is unknown, but it was begun in Shomu's reign, which extended from 724 to 749.

Songs of Two Cities—Nara

It is a peculiarity of Japanese poetry that frequently certain words are made to do double duty, and to become as it were the hinge or pivot upon which the thought turns. Thus in the original of this little piece, the "inexhaustible heavens" are the source at once of the snow-fall described and of the divine favors called down upon the empress. Thus image and idea are fused, the two making one; but the construction is, of course, illogical. If a literal translation had been given, the effect would be that of a mere play upon words. Yet there is an essential difference between the "pivot-word," as it has been called, and the pun, for the latter consists in the presentation simultaneously, and as though they were one and the same, of two radically different ideas, while the pivot-words of Japanese poetry are but a condensed form of the parallels in which Chinese as well as Hebrew poetry abounds. In another little ode, written after the removal of the capital from Nara to Kioto, the idea turns upon a comparison between the ninefold enclosures of the new palace, and the many-petalled flowers of the emperor's cherry-tree that had bloomed beside the steps to the throne-hall at Nara, and had been transplanted to his new residence. This meaning will appear, if we consider the words in *Italics* to refer to *both* those that precede and those that follow them. To repeat these "pivot-words" would

be to convert the little piece into a formal parallel
between the flowers and the palace.*

THE CHERRY-TREE TRANSPLANTED.

Nara's eightfold bloom,
Now ninefold walls surround it,
Fair and strong, new built ;
And sweeter far than ever
Its well-remembered fragrance.

The contrivance certainly conduces to brevity,
which, we are told, is the soul of wit ; but it has a
grotesque effect in English, and, along with other
peculiarities, usually makes it impossible to give anything like a close translation of Japanese poems. The
versification seems, at first sight, singularly easy to
imitate. The common form is in unrhymed verses
of five and seven syllables, alternating with an extra
line of seven syllables at the end. But Japanese is
practically without accent, which has so important an

* It was customary that the residence of the monarch should be
surrounded by those of the court nobles, the emperor's guards,
and personal attendants, disposed in various courts divided from
each other by walls. Thus the palace continued to resemble a
walled camp and to recall the stockade erected by Susanoō in
Izumo. This was eight-walled, it may be remembered, and it is
to be inferred from the poem that the palace at Nara had only
eight enclosures—the canonical number—while that later built at
Kioto had nine. The poem feigns that the transplanted cherry-
tree had also a new circle of petals added to its blossoms.

effect on English metres, and no recognized English rhythm reproduces the cadence of Japanese verse. For these reasons a wider license than ordinary is claimed for the imitations that follow.

But there is another sort of poetical composition, more curious still than the regular Japanese ode. This is written in Chinese ideograms, according to the elaborate rules of Chinese versification; but, pronounced as Japanese, it is only a sort of rhythmical prose. In explanation it may be enough to say that the Chinese signs have been used from a very early period in Japan to represent, not Chinese, but Japanese words. In the sort of composition referred to, the characters are arranged as in Chinese verse and can be read as such, but would often not be understood by a Chinaman because of the novel significations imposed upon many of them; while, read as Japanese, the meaning may be clear, but the piece is without poetic form. To those learned in both languages it is prose and poetry at once. But the privilege is inalienable; our alphabet makes anything of the sort impossible to us.

Apart from this, the following ode is strange enough to merit a moment's attention. It was written by the princely victim of the Empress Jito, before mentioned, on the evening of his execution, and gives us a curious insight into the beliefs that were current at Nara in the eighth century. The translation is close as to the sense, though not as to the form.

LINES WRITTEN BEFORE HIS EXECUTION, BY PRINCE OHOTSUNO.

See, the Golden Crow doth fly
To his hut beneath the West.
Hark, the drum ! This hour I die.

Where nor landlord is nor guest,
This hour I take the lonely road,
And enter on a hopeless quest.

Leaving for aye my soft abode,
Blindly, I seek the Fount unknown,
Whence first the Stream of Being flowed.

The Golden Crow is explained to mean the sun. The regular evening flight of the birds to their distant nests may have suggested the image ; and it is worth noting that, according to a legend in the "Kojiki," it was a friendly god in the form of a crow that led the Children of the Sun to the conquest of Yamato. It may be, therefore, that Ohotsuno intended some allusion to a version of the sun myth peculiar to that province. The *torii*, or so-called "gates," erected before Shintô temples, are believed to have been originally intended as perches for the sun, conceived as a great bird, to roost upon. The "soft abode" that the prince was about to quit was, of course, his body; and by the Unknown Fount he means the universal source of life to which, according to the Buddhist belief, all souls return at death, and from which they reissue in new shapes, until, at last, they attain Nirvana.

Such very cold comfort as might be derived from this philosophy was, it is pleasant to know, warmed for poor Ohotsuno by agreeable recollections. He had been a mighty hunter in his day, and could felicitate himself on the fact that he would die facing the scene of many of his exploits, the Lake of Iware, in the neighborhood of which he had been defeated and taken prisoner. As he neared the place of his execution the moon, on the point of being hidden behind the clouds, touched with a last ray the waters of the lake. The circumstance impressed him from its likeness to his own situation, and from it he drew this impromptu in the Japanese fashion:

> Iware, O beloved!
> Ere dark clouds close about me,
> Let my last glance fall
> On flocks of wild-fowl feeding,
> Where, in thy reeds, they gather.

He had often, we may suppose, gone hawking at nightfall upon the lake like the sportsmen in Hokusai's picture. The hawk was the only animal used in the chase. The dog, so far from being the hunters' friend, was hunted himself for practice when better game was lacking, a proceeding which may be commended to the attention of our Nimrods, who, when they have killed off every harmless wild creature, may perhaps make amends by killing their curs. Large game was stalked, or despatched with arrows, javelins, and hunting-knives, not without danger to life and limb at the finish; and a great hunt was a *battue* on a royal scale. In another Chinese poem of Ohotsuno that has come down to us, he describes a hunter's feast at evening in the forest.

THE RENDEZVOUS AFTER THE CHASE.

OHOTSUNO.

This morn we made a choice of men,
This eve a thousand mats we spread;
For now, the moon lights up the glen,
And clouds enwrap the mountain's head.
But still the topmost summits shine
All purple, 'gainst the evening blue:
Ho! comrades; here is meat and wine,
And merry be our rendezvous.

Love-songs and elegies form a large proportion of the odes of the " Myriad Leaves." The emotion expressed in them always has the ring of sincerity, but does not appear to have been very profound. A simple natural feeling was matter enough ; to voice it in few and fit words, the highest aim of art. The lyric might occasionally be spun out into a ballad ; but no attempt was ever made to connect ballad with ballad to form an epic.

Anything like a philosophical idea was repugnant to the Japanese muse, and was left to students of the Chinese mode like Ohotsuno, as a contrast to whose death-song may be given the simple elegy, affecting from its very simplicity, addressed by his enemy, Jito, to her deceased husband. The confusion of tenses, natural when one is moved by strong emotion, is in the original.

TO THE DEAD EMPEROR.

JITŌ TENNO.

Dread lord and master :
At evening thou wouldst gaze—
 Again at daybreak
Upon the Hill of Ghosts,
 Red with the maple :
To-day thou'dst gaze on it—
 Again to-morrow.

I, now, when evening falls,
 Lifting my eyes there,
Am overcome with sorrow ;
 Alone, at dawning,
The sleeve of my coarse robe
 Is never dry an instant.

The following (which may have been written on the same occasion) contains an allusion to the Buddhist doctrine that the soul, in separating finally from the body, gains admission to the world of real existences, this material world being essentially void and worthless. But it is altogether cast in a conventional mould, and is therefore inferior to Jito's simple *cri du cœur*.

THE EMPTY CHRYSALIS.

ANON.

Thou the spirit flown,
The empty shell am I, and
Cannot follow thee.
Last night in dream I saw thee,
But had no strength to follow.

Oh ! wert thou a gem
I'd set thee in my bracelet ;
Wert thou robe of serge
I never would disrobe me.
But last night, my prince,
I saw, but could not follow,
And had no joy in seeing.

It is time to turn to the chief poet of the " Myriad Leaves," the only one to whom Europeans would apply the epithet " great." Hitomaro is so much admired by his own countrymen that he has been made a god—one of the three gods of poetry. Yet more, he is incontestably the master-spirit of the trinity; for, of the other two, one is the genius of the pine-tree of Sumiyoshi, who, if he has inspired innumerable verses and kakemono in honor of conjugal fidelity, has written nothing himself, and the other is the Princess Sotoori, of whom little more is known than that she revealed herself as a goddess to some good people of the province of Kii in 724, three hundred years after her death. The circumstantial account which we have of Hitomaro's apotheosis reveals to us one of the ways in which public opinion made itself felt in old Japan. The poet, though accounted noble, was of low grade and obscure birth. A native of the province of Iwami, on the western seaboard, he appears to have been received at the court of the Empress Jito in the capacity of tutor to the heir-apparent, Prince Hinami, and, after the latter's early death, as a retainer of Prince Takaichi. In the latter's service he must have resided some time at Nara, where he may have listened to the first notes of the great bell, and witnessed the erection of the colossal Buddha. Late in life he returned to his province, where he had been provided with a comfortable post. He died there A.D. 737.

His fame, at first overshadowed by that of the princely and imperial poets of his time, continued to grow for centuries after his death. Toward the close of the classic period his songs, distinguished for their natural flow of feeling and their original and often striking imagery, were the models most appreciated by the tasteful but less gifted writers of the day. To one of these admirers, Fujiwara no Kanefusa, more celebrated as an artist than as a poet, Hitomaro condescended to appear in a dream, and the enthusiastic disciple, well knowing that no authentic likeness existed, painted the vision from memory and presented the " portrait " to the emperor. Another enthusiast, Akisuyé, obtained permission to have a copy made for him, and instituted a yearly festival in its honor on the anniversary of Hitomaro's death. Before this, legend had been busy with the scanty records of the poet's life. It was fabled that he was sprung from some mikado of the mythical period; and that when found by his foster-father (a common soldier) under a persimmon-tree, the babe lisped in numbers and claimed to be able, by song, to make the winds and the tides move at his pleasure. The emperor, himself an admirer of Hitomaro, and perhaps influenced by this legend, when he heard of the honors rendered by Akisuyé, set aside the taxes of a village to defray the cost of a more imposing annual ceremony, and formally recognized the poet as a god. A shrine was built and dedicated, which was in time replaced by the fine temple at Akashi near Kobé, where his worship is still maintained with yearly rites and sacrifices.

The little that is really known of Hitomaro is derived from the notes to his poems in the " Myriad Leaves." The subject of the following lines appears to have been a pretty waitress at an inn in Karu, at that time a noted pleasure resort near the capital. It is a pity that we cannot fancy her, like her successors of to-day, bringing to her courtly customer seated under the wistarias, a tiny porcelain cup of fragrant tea; for neither porcelain nor the tea-shrub had as yet been introduced into Japan. The divine Hitomaro's august tipple was doubtless hot rice whiskey.

THE WELL-TROD WAY TO KARU.

HITOMARO.

Oftener had I gone
The well-trod way to Karu,
 All for the dear sake
Of a fair maid who dwelt there,
 But, if folk had seen
Me morning, noon, and night there,
 The tale had spread apace,
For many a friend had borne it.

So I hid my heart,
Like hermit in a valley.
 " Tendrils of the vine
Will twine again when parted,"

63

Sunrise Stories

Thought I.   But my love
Fell like a leaf in autumn—
    Sank like sun at eve,
Or moon behind a cloud bank.

    Ah ! when came the news,
No word nor motion had I,
    Till, urgèd by despair,
I took the way to Karu.
    Once more I passed her gate,
But heard no whispered welcome ;
    Nowhere in the throng
Saw I the face I craved for.

    Oh ! then, the crowd forgot,
Her treasured name escaped me,
    As I my sleeve stood waving.

The nature of the indiscretion into which grief had led our poet was at once understood by his contemporaries, who used the flowing sleeve, worn by both sexes, to express their emotions, which appear to have been much more lively with the ancient Japanese than with their descendants.   It was the sleeve that was wet with tears, "like the rock in the open sea," when the wearer gave way to grief.   It was with a wave of the sleeve that friends and lovers bade one another farewell at parting.   Hitomaro, therefore, could not have more plainly published the state of his heart.   But we need not suppose that flirtations of this sort led often to serious love-making.   That they were lightly begun, the subjoined ode shows; and, no doubt, they were often as lightly ended.

RED LACQUER BRIDGE.

ANON.

O'er Red Lacquer Bridge,
Across the Katashiha,
  Goes a fair maid dressed
All in blue and crimson.
  Alone ! I wish I knew
If she's ever lonely,
  And where she lives ; but, hold !
I'll ask herself to tell me.

Nothing great is to be expected of an affair begun in that fashion. But Hitomaro, though it is known that he had left behind him in his native Iwaki another mistress, whom he also celebrated in song, was evidently deeply smitten by the pretty girl of Karu ; and it may have been she who caused him the sleepless night described in one of the most admired of his short odes.

The Yamadori, or mountain pheasant, it may be well to say, is noted in poetry as an image of anxious affection and solicitude. The male bird is said to walk slowly to and fro, dragging its long wing-feathers as if wounded, to attract the attention of the sportsman when its nest is in danger. As used here it is to suggest that in the long night hours the same moments seem to return over and over again. The word here translated "foot-sore" is the "pivot word" of the original. It means to drag the feet, to be fatigued; but, as applied to mountains it also conveys the notion of the long succession of the foot-hills.

> As the trailing wings
> Of the wounded pheasant
> On the foot-sore hills,
> Pass and repass the moments
> Of the weary vigil.

But Hitomaro had possibly other causes for sleeplessness. He cannot but have seen at Nara that Buddhism, along with many benefits, had brought not a few troubles upon the country. His doubts seem to be painted in his little picture of a moonrise, which, nevertheless, is nothing but a succession of images.

GOOD AND EVIL.

HITOMARO.

> O'er yon shadowy Alp,
> Serene, the full moon rises.
> Rises yon dun cloud,
> Upon the night-breeze soaring,
> To reach and overcast it?

In fact, in Hitomaro's day the cloud had already risen that was to overshadow the glories of Nara.

Songs of Two Cities—Nara

The daughter of Shomu and his consort, Koken, who became empress in 749, was born in 716. Once on the throne, she appears to have set out deliberately to copy the Empress Jito. After a reign of ten years she placed on the throne the Emperor Junnin, only to depose him a few years later and exile him to the island of Awaji, where he was killed in an attempt at escape. During her second reign her relations with certain Buddhist priests caused immense scandal, from which both religion and the Court suffered. One of her favorites she wished to make emperor; but these plans were balked, and threats of rebellion brought the empress to her senses. Still, it is believed that it was partly on this account that Nara was deserted by her successor, Kuanmu, who in 795 removed the capital to the neighboring province of Yamashiro. The poet Sakimaro's verses on the occasion give voice to the regrets of the inhabitants, who had come to look upon Nara as the permanent capital of the country.

THE LAMENT FOR NARA.

SAKIMARO.

Ne'er has Yamato
Been kingless or lawless.
 Since gods came from heaven
To rule in her borders.

Sunrise Stories

Never, so deemed we,
Should Nara be kingless
    While ages unnumbered
Passed over her dwellings.

    Spring on Mikasa
Saw cherry-trees blooming,
    White, where the mist wreath
Lay dim on the mountain.
    Autumn, Ikoma
Made white with the hoar frost,
    And heard the stag belling
In flowering copses.

    Would that forever
The hills might look down on
    Thy broad streets laid out for
Brave warriors to dwell in.
    Would that thy glory
Might, lasting as heaven's,
    Fail but when faileth
The frame universal.

But Majesty speaketh,
    And Nara's deserted.
Men flee her gates
    As the birds flee ere winter.
No more voice of herald
    Or neighing of horses
Resounds in the streets
    Of the desolate city.

VII

SONGS OF TWO CITIES—KIOTO

No great statue of Buddha, like that at Nara, presided over the Emperor Kuanmu's City of Peace, as he, at first, called his new capital. Instead, an effigy of a full-armed warrior was buried in a hill outside the walls, to act as protecting deity. This curious reversion to barbaric usages shows that Buddhism had encountered a notable check. It recovered, however, and its priests soon regained most of the power that they had enjoyed in civil as well as in religious matters. The new city, lying in a fertile plain, agreeably watered by many little streams, all running into the Yodogawa, the outlet of Lake Biwa, was, in time, surrounded by a complete girdle of monasteries and temples. On the western outskirts, not far from the palace, lay the monastery of Omuro, which became a favorite place of retreat for descendants of the imperial house. Near by was the already ancient temple of Koriūji, founded by Shotoku Taishi. A little farther afield was the great temple of Saga. To the south lay the temple of Toji, where envoys from China and Korea were lodged, and where Kōbō Daishi preached and wrought miracles. To the east was Kiomidzudera, built over the cascade where the goddess of Mercy had visited the hermit Enshin in his hut. Shotoku Taishi's pagoda, and Kodaiji, whose Founder's Hall is now ceiled with panels from Hideyoshi's war-junk and his wife's travelling-carriage, lay in the same direction. On the hills overlooking Lake Biwa had been established, more than a century before, the famous rival monasteries of Miidera and Hieisan. Literature, which had begun to show symptoms of decline toward the end of the Nara period, revived, and was zealously cultivated in these institutions and at the Court, which now began to form itself into an exclusive and over-refined society, apart from the more active elements of the nation.

The invention of a new style of phonetic writing (attributed to Kōbō Daishi) made it possible to write Japanese without any knowledge of either the spoken or the written language of China. Hence, in addition to the continuations of the national chronicles, still written in the Chinese manner, an abundant prose literature in the form of diaries, "mirror histories," that is, minute and faithful records of everyday occurrences, and monogatari, or prose romances, mostly the work of women, began to appear.

The earliest of these romances were built up, on the system already described, about short poetical pieces which they professed to explain. Thus the "Romance of Ise," so called because its author was daughter of a governor of that province, is simply a more or less fanciful commentary on the odes of the poet Narihira, relating in detail the adventures which are supposed to have given rise to the poems. The ode itself gradually became restricted to the thirty-one syllable form, and lost in emotional warmth, but gained in point and brilliancy.

What the "Myriad Leaves" is to the poetry of Nara, the "Collection of Songs, Old and New," is to that of Kioto. It was undertaken, at the instance of the Emperor Daigo, by the poet Tsurayuki and three assistants. Tsurayuki's preface is of considerably more interest than his own poems, in which he rings without end the changes on "snow blossoms" and "blossom snow," "foam blossoms," and so on. He endeavored to classify the Japanese odes in the categories recognized by the Chinese, and, more successfully, to characterize shortly the peculiar manner of each poet. Narihira's verse, according to this first of Japanese critics, is laden with meanings which the words hardly suffice to express. It is like a closed blossom that holds its color and its fragrance in reserve for him who will give it patient attention. The Lady Komachi's style is querulous and delicate, "like a pretty woman worn away by illness." On

the other hand, the devotion to verse of the good
Bishop Henzeu seems to him but an artificial flame
for a mere painted image ; and Kuromochi, a famous
poet in his day, is rated for his clumsy archaisms as
a " beggarly fagot-gatherer, resting by chance under
the shadow of the blossoms."

The modern student will be inclined to think that
the qualities for which Narihira is praised are common
to many other artificers of the short ode.   In Chinese
didactic poetry * the idea is first suggested vaguely,
in a sort of prefatory stanza, by some pleasing image
frequently drawn from natural scenery, and, the mind
thus prepared to receive it, the moral, which is everything to the practical Chinese, is stated in plain and
vigorous terms.   But their more artistic cousins
elaborate the image and give but the faintest and
politest hint of a moral lesson.   And in numberless instances the aim of the poet is, like that of the
musician, merely to induce a certain mood in the
hearer.   The difference is to be ascribed to the
elasticity of the Japanese mind, which more easily
reaches the plane of ideas than the Chinese ; and to
a peculiar dislike of what is superfluous and redun-
dant.   To pass lightly and quickly from point to point
and leave the reader in a mood to dwell upon the
subject, seems to be their usual aim.   In the sub-

* See Dr. Legge's translation of the Shih King.

joined ode of Narihira's, the poet ironically declares that spring would be indeed delightful if there were no blossoms, for to the stress of production he ascribes the storms and rain that accompany the season. The reader is credited with penetration enough to discover the hidden meaning, which is that the poet's spring-time would also have to be deprived of its bloom, if aged censors, fond of quiet and decorum, had to be satisfied.

THE SPRING LIKE ITS POET.

NARIHIRA.

Charming were the Spring,
Unmarred by tears or tempests,
If the flowers ne'er bloomed.
Unfeared were, then, its coming ;
Its going unregretted.

Henzeu, whom Tsurayuki held in such slight esteem, was very successful in this way, putting a sermon into a few pleasant verses. That he also had original ideas in theology is certain, if our interpretation of his ode on the lotus be correct.

GRACE AND GOOD-NATURE.

HENZEU SOZYO.

Pure as pure can be,
The flower of the lotus !
Say not, fairer shines
The dew that falls from Heaven,
Into its open chalice.

It is not always easy to seize the elusive thought which these little pieces denote rather than express. Here the dew signifies supernatural grace, while the lotus-flower, springing from the black mud of the ditch, is a perfect symbol of natural goodness of heart unaffected by evil conditions, which the Bishop appears to have prized as highly. Henzeu was grandson of the founder of Kioto. His ordination took place late in life, and his son, born before his entry into religion, became the noted abbot and poet, Sosei. Some of the best effusions of the latter may compare with Herrick's for delicate and kindly humor. His thoughts run mostly on his garden and his convent. The chattering of those " little monks," the sparrows, and the mischief that they work among the flowers, inspired him with the idea of reading a lesson to those under his charge, who, like monks and children everywhere, were always ready to lay the blame at others' doors that properly belonged to themselves. Accordingly, in remonstrating with the culprits, he is really conveying a sly hint to his bonzes.

TO THE BIRDS THAT SCATTERED THE BLOSSOMS.

SOSEI HŌSHI.

Whom, now, so noisily,
Would ye incriminate?
None but yourselves it was,
Restlessly fluttering,
Shook down the blossoms.

Songs of Two Cities—Kioto

But the rough winds work even worse havoc among the plum- and cherry-trees than the birds, and, in launching anathemas against them, the brave abbot imagines himself one of the militant saints of an earlier age, when there were not only unruly monks, but blood-thirsty bandits also, to deal with. In a companion piece to the last, he humorously pictures himself a valiant champion of the Church, like the great Kōbō Daishi, who once put to rout the brigands that, in his day, infested the environs of Kioto, as will be told in another chapter.

ON THE WINDS THAT RAVISHED THE BLOSSOMS.

SOSEI.

What wild cave hides them,
Robber winds, plunderers?
Tell me! I'll face them—
And lecture them soundly,
For raiding my garden.

Though the thirty-one syllable ode was the form preferred by most of the poets of Kioto,* the Chinese style of versification was not abandoned. In fact, it was more than ever cultivated, owing to the accelerated influx of Buddhist monks driven out of China

* In some of the imitations here given the crime, unpardonable in Japanese, is committed of making the stanza consist of only twenty-eight syllables.

by the persecutions of the Thang emperors. Forty-five thousand temples and monasteries are said to have been destroyed in a single reign. These persecutions sent many, who might otherwise have chosen a conventual life, into the wilds, to live as hermits. Sometimes, keeping together in little bands, they were known as the "Friends of the Bamboo Grove." The custom was extended to Japan, and we may assume that this kind of life was not without its attractions. Its praises are sung by the bonze Chizō, a contemporary of Sosei :

THE LAND OF RIGHT REASON.

CHIZŌ.

Would you know the place where Reason flourishes?
Go seek it in the Land of Humanity and Wisdom.
There, the air is pure, the hills and the streams are pleasant,
Strong is the breeze and laden with pleasant odors.

Now the small birds' nests show through denuded branches,
The wild-geese on their pond intone their chants autumnal ;
The Friends to the Grove retired rejoice in the changing sea-
	sons
And reck not of shifting tides of men's esteem and censure.

There is a legend, often illustrated by artists, of a Friend who became an out-and-out recluse, retiring to a small island, the bridge leading to which he vowed never to recross. But two of his former companions visiting him, engaged him in a conversation which he found so agreeable that he unconsciously prolonged his walk with them beyond the fateful bridge. Upon which the two old cocks fell a-laughing, and the would-be anchorite, laughing also, returned to the community.

For the terror of the wilderness shown in the ancient stories, Buddhism had succeeded in substituting a feeling of intimacy with wild nature. Much of our modern enjoyment of landscape may be traced to monachism. In Japan, the feeling profoundly influenced all the later literature and art of the country. The majority of the nation were, however, as yet, far from showing this love of retirement and of wildness. The old pagan dislike and dread of solitude was still uppermost at the time of which we are now writing. A member of the Minamoto warrior clan, whom the departure of his comrades to winter quarters had left alone at his post in a snow-bound mountain village, is the author of an ode which may serve as a contrast to Chizō.

WINTER SOLITUDE.

MUNEYUKI.

Hateful is this life
Cut off by winter's hosts, in
Lonely hamlet penned ;
Green leaves and friendly faces
All withered, all departed !

Even the hermit and the wanderer by choice sometimes found that they paid too much for their advantages, as appears to have been the case with the anonymous author of the two following odes, which appear to belong together:

THE EXILE.

All alone, I sang—
'Til sickness came upon me,
  In my little den,
Warmed with a stick of charcoal.
  Now the exile fain
Would to his own land turn,
But, still, the wind blows onward.

Pleasant 'twere to wake,
Although from pleasant slumber,
  With the joyous sound,
The sound of water rushing
  'Gainst the speedy ship,
To see the bright waves pass,
The dear, dark hills draw nearer!

But a lighter and more cheerful turn of mind, and a delight in natural beauty of a quiet sort, had become general. Narihira might see portents dire in the reflection of the crimson foliage of the maples in the stream swollen by autumn floods, and be reminded of Susanoö's slaying of the Dragon:

Tats'ta, brimming full,
Rolls between drenched banks, reddened
As though with slaughter huge,
A grimmer sight, I ween, than
Izumo's bloodied river.

But to Michizané the maples of Mount Tamuké suggest but a novel reason for not paying his temple dues. It was customary, each autumn, to bring offerings of figured silks to the Shintô shrine upon the mountain, which was celebrated for the beauty of its maple forests at that season ; and Michizané, who was too honest to grow rich, hints that the gods might very well content themselves with the productions of nature's loom.

THE MAPLES.

SUGAWARA NO MICHIZANE.

'Tis hardly for poor me
To bring a beggar's gift, when
Tam'keyama spreads
Miles of red maple damask
Before the glad immortals.

The poet is now himself an immortal, having been deified by an admiring people, not, like Hitomaro, for his poetry, nor for his services to the Empire as a statesman, but for his skill in calligraphy. It does not appear that he will take autumn leaves for Kioto brocade from his worshippers.

Sunrise Stories

The taste for natural beauty had already led to a considerable development of landscape-gardening. Monasteries and palaces had their grounds laid out in artful imitation of natural scenery. Most of them had their "Moon-gazing arbors," where enthusiasts often passed half the night composing verses and sipping *saké*. To this custom we owe some verses in the Chinese style by the Emperor Montoku, which may (not inappropriately) end this sketch of the poets of Kioto.

THE VOYAGE OF THE MOON.

MONTOKU TENNO.

A sycamore boat on a sea of mist,
  The moon sails, coasting by isles of amber;
And trembles, now, in my cup, I wist,
  And now stands poised o'er my leafy chamber.

The shadows break on the wave, afar,
  Cool blows the breeze from the forest, yonder;
And forth, convoyed by many a star,
  In the open heaven, she goes—a wonder!

VIII

THE VOYAGE HOME FROM TOSA

MONOGATARI

Tsurayuki, who edited the songs of old Kioto, has another claim to recognition as author of a serio-comic narrative of a short voyage, which has never ceased to be admired as a model of classical Japanese. Of prose compositions of its kind, the "Tosa Diary" is first both in point of date and of merit. It is a lively account of a tedious journey. The slow progress and rough accommodations of Lamb's "Old Margate Hoy" were as steam and a first-cabin passage to those that Tsurayuki's chartered junk afforded. The delays and discomforts of the voyage would hardly be found amusing by a traveller of to-day; but, like Horace on his journey to Brundusium, our author was competent to extract pleasure out of misery, and wit out of dulness.

Taking advantage of the new phonetic characters, at first used by the ladies of the Court, he sets up the pretence that his diary is written by a woman. In this way he finds occasion to praise his administration, now at an end, of the affairs of the province of Tosa, and to speak of himself as a man of considerable ability, who had known how to win the hearts of his people. By this ingenious mystification he is also enabled to quote his own poetry, and, in general, to advertise his good qualities of mind, heart, and person. To strike a balance, he mentions, with feminine circumlocution, that on his taking leave of the new governor appointed to succeed him, "their parting utterances were exceedingly amusing, owing to the fact that both were somewhat maudlin from over-conviviality." *

The journey began, nominally, on the twenty-first day of the twelfth month, at eight o'clock in the evening. But all of the next day was taken up in praying to the gods for a safe passage, and in a feast on the beach at which everybody, both high and low, became tipsy. The next day and the three following were spent in the same manner, and everybody belonging to the ship, even to the children, roamed unsteadily about the beach, their feet continually making the sign for ten (x). In the midst of this disorder, Tsurayuki's little daughter, who had made the outward voyage with him, died suddenly, and the actual separation from Tosa was saddened by

* Log of a Japanese Journey. By Flora Best Harris. Meadville, Pa. 1891.

The Voyage Home from Tosa

the thought that she would never again behold her home at the capital, where she was born. The brother of the new governor and some friends, galloping along the shore, overtook the ship on the evening of the first day's voyage, and all went ashore to feast and compose verses. The parting speeches were interminable. The guests became more and more emotional, and found it more and more difficult to express their feelings in suitable language. But the rude sailors, incapable of understanding their state of mind and heart, cut matters short, and, calling out that the company must surely have drunk sufficiently, and that they must take advantage of the fair wind and high tide, summoned the passengers aboard. But they continued to sing so melodiously that they shook the dust from the ceiling of the cabin, and the clouds in heaven, pausing in their course, rocked themselves gently to and fro, in time to the measure.

On the twenty-eighth day they put into a port where they passed New-Year's-Day and several days thereafter. The people of the place brought them presents of fresh provisions, which put them in a quandary, for they had nothing on board with which to make a return. So well victualled were they, nevertheless, that " the vulgar crew made drums of their overfull stomachs, and went about beating

them," and cut such other grotesque antics that the
sea, mother of monsters, had never beheld the like.
The better-behaved passengers, guests of the master
of the vessel, passed their time in moon-gazing and
composing verses.

On the ninth day of the New Year, the friends
who had been following them along the shore took
leave in earnest, and the ship put out to sea, to make
the passage to Awa. That night, being out of sight
of land, the women and children, lying in the hold,
were greatly alarmed, and the author, in his assumed
character, feigns to have shared in their distress.
But the sailors kept their courage up, singing comic
songs, and toward morning they got into harbor.
There they stayed a day, putting to sea again by
moonlight, while the passengers slept. The thirteenth day, again passed in harbor, turning out fine,
though it had been stormy in the morning, they
went ashore, dressed (that is to say, the women) in
their best scarlet robes, which they had not dared to
wear on shipboard for fear of exciting the jealousy of
the sea-gods.

They did not get under way again until the seventeenth, when they rowed out by morning twilight,
Tsurayuki remarking on the beauty of the shifting
tints of sky and sea in the blended light of dawn and
the full moon. But, just after daybreak, a black

The Voyage Home from Tosa

cloud came up, and the sailors insisted on turning
back. A snow-storm that lasted for several days
followed, and the miserable passengers were fain to
beguile the time by composing verses as wretched as
their condition.

On the twenty-first, the numerous vessels detained
by the storm put out together, looking like autumn
leaves strewn over the face of the ocean. The sight
of the waves breaking on some rocks in the distance,
led the writer (Tsurayuki still playing the part of a
woman) to conjure up visions of shipwreck and pirates, and all sorts of ocean perils. In mockery,
doubtless, of some well-known effusion of the sort, he
fancies his hair turning white with terror :

> Headman, oh ! headman
> Of the island, out yonder,
>   Tell me, I pray you,
> If my hairs be the whiter,
> Or the foam on the billows ?

he writes, and playfully asks the skipper to deliver
the ode to the person addressed, and bring back an
answer.

The fear of pirates seems to have spread among the
crew, and prayers were offered up to the gods and to
Buddha. From the twenty-third to the twenty-sixth
the vessel was in some port of the province of Awa ;
but, getting word that pirates were actually planning

to seize them, they set sail at midnight. Passing a small shrine, situated on a promontory, bits of bright-colored silks were scattered on the waves, as offerings to the sea-gods. An old woman of Awaji, one of the passengers, awakened by the flapping of the sails, composed a stanza in which they were said to be clapping their hands in their joy at being hoisted. But they were hauled down again next day, and the poor passengers, out of all patience, snapped their fingers in disgust, as well they might, and, their poetic vein being quite exhausted, were driven to take refuge in sleep.

On the first day of the second month, having crossed the strait from Awa, they reached the coast of Izumi, and, the wind failing, the sailors were obliged to drag the junk along the shore by ropes. Even this slow progress they were soon obliged to relinquish by a return of stormy weather, which the sailors attributed to some caprice of the god of Sumi-yoshi. Silk shreds were again scattered abroad, but the tempest did not abate; on the contrary, the waves grew higher and threatened to drive the vessel ashore. It was plain that the god was not to be appeased except by the sacrifice of something of more value. In this emergency the author threw into the sea a mirror, an object which, to a woman, is dearer than one of her eyes. "A sorrowful thing it was to

The Voyage Home from Tosa

do," but the sea at once became as smooth as the polished metal.

It was on the sixth that they entered the mouth of the Yodogawa; but now the shallows in the river detained them, and the vessel had to be lightened. They themselves left her at Yamazaki, and travelled the remaining five miles to the capital by the more expeditious bullock cart. Tsurayuki noticed that the pictures on the articles for sale in the shops were the same as when he left. It was night when he entered Kioto, after having been fifty-four days in making a journey of less than two hundred miles. His house and garden, which he had left in the care of a neighbor, were in ruins. The dismal sight, and the thought of the little girl who was born in the place, and whose fate it was never to return there, overwhelmed him with grief, made more poignant by the indifference of his shipmates, who now left him with a few careless expressions of sympathy. In his dejection he records the intention to destroy the manuscript of his diary; but, since the resolution was not carried out, we are perhaps justified in regarding it as part of the fiction so ingeniously kept up throughout the narrative.

The "Tosa Nikki" was followed by a multitude of efforts in the same manner, diaries and "mirror histories," of the greatest value to the antiquary from their numerous and detailed descriptions of ancient manners, but which need not detain us from a consideration of the more generally interesting monogatari.

Various forms of prose narrative are included under this term, but in all an element of fiction is openly admitted. Some of the more celebrated are but artistically embellished biographies; others are fairy-tales; still others are historical romances, in which the fiction sometimes serves only as a setting for authentic documents. Written as a rule by women, they often betray the slightness of the hold that serious continental beliefs had obtained on the minds of their authors and readers. The facts of contemporary life and history, the refinements of Chinese light literature, and the crudities of native legend, furnish the matter of these romances, which usually display a critical and ironical turn of mind, a somewhat affected appreciation of beauty, and a very real dislike of being bored by stock phrases and situations known in advance.

"The Bamboo Cutter," * the most ancient of these compositions, is referred by some authorities to the first half of the ninth century, which would make it antedate Tsurayuki's Diary and the collection of "Songs, Old and New." It is a fairy-story, possibly

* Taketori Monogatari.

The Voyage Home from Tosa

of Chinese origin, but told in a spirit of raillery that reminds one of the "Moral Tales" of the witty Count Hamilton.

An old bamboo-cutter, who had finished his day's work on the hills near Lake Biwa, and tied up his fagot, bethought him to cut an extra cane to serve for a staff on his way down the snow-clad slopes of the mountain. Astonished to see light streaming from the incision made by his knife, he carefully laid open the hollow joint and found within it an infant from whose tiny body came the supernatural radiance. He took the prodigy home, and she grew to be a famous beauty. Suitors came from all directions, and even from the Imperial City. But not caring to accept the addresses of any of them, the Bamboo Maiden set them impossible tasks to perform, pretending that her object was to test the sincerity of their professions. One soon returned with an old silver cup, gray from oxidation, which he had bought at an extravagant price from a Buddhist monk as the legendary vessel that he had been required to discover. But the sharp-witted maiden immediately scoured it, and brought out an inscription showing that it was of comparatively modern manufacture. Another had been despatched to seek an enchanted island where grew a golden tree bearing jewels for fruit. This gentleman came back, after a longer in-

terval, with a moving tale of shipwreck and disaster
and a branch which he had had made by a jeweller
in Kioto. His golden branch had not the requisite
magic virtues, however, and a sharp cross-examina-
tion developed serious flaws in his story. A third,
himself deceived by a merchant into buying for a
great price a blue-fox skin, said to be uninflammable,
saw his gift consigned to the flames, where it perished in an instant; and a fourth, the only suitor
who had honestly attempted the task assigned him,
had the worst luck of all, for he fell from the sheer
rock that he was to scale and broke his neck.

The fame of the wise but dangerous beauty at last
reached the Emperor, and he set out in his august
bullock cart to visit her. A flame at once sprang
up between the two; but the maiden was proof
against even the attractions of love in a palace. Having fulfilled the period of her exile, she returned to
the moon, whence she had come, leaving an example
of obstinate virtue, which, unfortunately, is "unap-
proachable by mortal women."

"The Uninhabited Forest" is a collection of
tales of a similar kind, ascribed to the same period.
In it there appear talking beasts, and a magic harp,
and a mysterious stranger who teaches the hero the
secrets of the instrument. The wit of some of the
tales is of a broader character. The hero of Torikai-

The Voyage Home from Tosa

baya ("What if I Were to Change Them?") is a perplexed father who brings up his effeminate son as a girl, and his tomboy daughter as a boy, with results more amusing than edifying. There is a strong family likeness between these early tales and those of the "Arabian Nights," and it is possible that some of the plots may have made their way to Japan from Persia. But in their present dress they are as thoroughly Japanese as the odes of the "Myriad Leaves." As a rule, however little we may admire the conduct of the heroes and heroines, their adventures are related with the utmost propriety of expression. This is pre-eminently the case with the "Romance of Genji," the most celebrated of them all.

Madame Murasaki, its author, was of the Fujiwara family, the noblest, after the Imperial House, in Japan. While serving as maid of honor to the Empress, she was commanded to write an interesting story for a princess who had been sent to fill the place of High Priestess at the shrine of Amaterasu in Ise. This little person—the "Sacred Virgin" was usually of a tender age—had exhausted all the limited stock of fiction then in existence, and had written to her Majesty to procure her something new. The subject of Prince Genji's amatory adventures was rather a curious choice to make in the circumstances; but, as we have said, no objection can be taken to the

author's treatment of it. Her choice of a retreat
throws a still more curious light on the manners of
the day, for she retired to a Buddhist monastery to
write her romance, and, being apparently short of
parchment, used the back of one of the Sacred Rolls,
the Mahaprajnaparamita,* on which to jot down
two of her chapters. The identical roll which she
later copied out to replace the one she had desecrated
is still preserved in the room where it was written, at
Ishiyamadera. The place overlooks the narrows
where Lake Biwa issues in the Yodogawa.

Murasaki had advanced ideas of the utility and
importance of fiction, and her work may almost be
spoken of as "a novel with a purpose." "Histories," she makes her hero say, "are but dry records
of events, and are usually partisan and one-sided;
but romances furnish a true and vivid picture of
social conditions. They are fictions, but not altogether; the essential thing about them being that
their authors, not pretending to historical accuracy,
are at liberty to put before us only what is best in
life, when their object is to display the good, and the
most comical when they wish to amuse." She is
credited by some of her admirers with uncommon
political insight; but her understanding of politics is
that of most of her sex, who believe in their hearts

* Or, rather, the Chinese translation.

that the sole object of human society is to support a court. She had the good sense not to attempt many male characters, and those she has introduced are treated frankly from the feminine point of view; but her sketches of the women who succeed one another so rapidly in the affections of her fickle hero are altogether admirable. The book begins with an account of the hero's birth and childhood, which we pass over, and begin with the chapter celebrated by Sir Edwin Arnold, which describes a conversation between Genji and his intimates one rainy night in the palace.

IX

A RAINY NIGHT ENTERTAINMENT

THE " Splendid Genji " was the son of the Emperor Seiwa, little mentioned in history, who reigned
peacefully from A.D. 859 to 877. Already, at this
date, the more powerful of the noble families shared
the administrative offices between them, and had established the principle that no member of the Imperial house should take an active part in affairs ; a most
convenient rule for *fainéant* princes and ambitious
subjects. Genji's mother came of a clan which could
muster but few adherents ; and, as a pretender to the
throne, he would be a mere pawn in the game played
by these unscrupulous intriguers. For this reason,
and because he showed signs of uncommon talent, his
careful father cut him off from the succession, and,
with admirable foresight, had him married at a very
early age, and solemnly set apart to found a new
family. In the main, his previsions turned out to be
correct. Genji, though on the surface of a careless
and pleasure-loving disposition, showed some ability
as a general, and a remarkable aptitude for political

A Rainy Night Entertainment

wire-pulling, and rose, some years after his father's
death, to be the actual ruler, as regent, of the Empire.
Three centuries later the Gen, or Minamoto, clan, of
which he is regarded as the founder, furnished to
Japan its first dynasty of hereditary shoguns. Murasaki portrays her hero as a reckless seeker of adventures, a sort of Japanese Don Juan, whose numerous
and devoted friends, whose good luck, patience, and
address barely suffice to bring him safely through the
numerous scrapes in which he involves himself. In
one of her best chapters, she shows him, at the outset
of his career, surrounded by his companions, to whose
good advice he turns a deaf ear, but whose question-
able experiences he finds highly interesting.*

It was a stormy night in May; the Court was keeping a fast; and Genji and his brother-in-law, Chiujio,
were amusing themselves by looking over old letters
in the former's apartment in the palace. The two
were fast friends, owing in good part to the fact that
they were in very much the same situation; each
having been married, for reasons of state, to a lady
for whom he felt no affection. Chiujio, older than
Genji, and freer in his movements, had already found
means of distraction. But he desired that his penny-
worth of observation might be of service to his sister's

* What follows is much condensed. A few details necessary to
an understanding of the context have been added.

husband, and he sometimes made his company burdensome by volunteering good advice, based on his own experience, which, however, he was usually discreet enough to keep to himself.

"Truly," said he, on this occasion, as he returned the letters that he had been glancing over, "perfection is hard to find in the sex. Every woman has her failing, and pursuit, even when successful, but leads to disappointment."

"But, at least, you will allow to each of them a good trait or two," suggested Genji. To which Chiujio gallantly replied that if such were not the case no one would ever be deceived; and, seeing that Genji was more than usually attentive, he went on to divide all womankind into classes, and to demonstrate categorically that in none of them could man hope to discover the ideal object of his desires. "Those best favored, and of the highest birth," he remarked, "are so strictly guarded as to be unavailable as subjects of experiment and comparison. The low-born and ugly are hardly worth the trouble. Thus the field is narrowed to the middle class, which, indeed, contains individuals who may, for a time, captivate a man's reason, but which, in the nature of things, can really produce only middling specimens."

"Admirable," cried Genji. "But, tell me this. In which of your three divisions would you put the

A Rainy Night Entertainment

decayed gentlewomen, and the parvenues? It seems
to me that, from different points of view, both may
appear to belong to the highest."

Chiujio was about to reply, but, just at this point,
the sliding screens were pushed apart, and the Master
of the Horse and the Secretary to the Master of the
Ceremonies * entered the room, and he referred the
question to the former.

After meditating for a moment, the Master of the
Horse seated himself upon a cushion, and with becoming gravity delivered his opinion. "Poor gentlewomen, and those newly ennobled, belong," said he,
"to Chiujio's middle class, in which class, too, I
would include the daughters of deputy-governors of
provinces, who are now and then introduced at Court,
and are frequently not without attractions. But, as
for perfection, if found at all, it will perhaps be in
the most unlikely conditions. Within some ruinous
enclosure, choked with weeds, and forgotten by the
world," he opined, "there may possibly be discovered a charming creature, of unimagined beauty,
refined and gentle, an accomplished poetess and
musician. But then, her father may be a robust and
stern old man, and her brothers truculent and repulsive bullies. Still, should such an one exist, she

* Most of the characters in the book are spoken of by their titles,
not by their names.

would," he thought, " deserve the attention of all but the most exalted young gentlemen."

At this, Mr. Secretary, who also had taken a seat by the lamp, was observed to change countenance. In fact, he imagined that he detected in the speech a covert allusion to his own pretty sisters, who were suffered by him to vegetate in poverty. Genji, perceiving his embarrassment, and divining the cause, set him at ease by uttering a few words about the extraordinary conditions attached to this supposititious case ; and then, seeing that the speaker was preparing to launch forth upon a long moral discourse, shut his eyes and composed himself to sleep.

But the Master of the Horse was now mounted upon his hobby, and nothing could shake him off. He gravely pursued his course, and described in turn the mock-modest woman, the over-sentimental, the dull and unsympathetic. He pictured the virago who fiercely berates her wretched partner for some fancied inconstancy, and her rarer opposite, who instead of complaining of the annoyances to which a thoughtless husband may have subjected her, runs away to the mountains, or, worse yet, to a convent, where she soon learns to regret the world she has left behind.

Carried away by his own eloquence, the speaker, who had shortly before been made Doctor of Literature, and who was " showing off his fine feathers,"

A Rainy Night Entertainment

announced the novel principle that, in women as in
the arts, mere cleverness, fashionable extravagance,
and display should not be accounted admirable, and,
having lost himself in the mazes of his rhetoric, suddenly stopped short. To cover his confusion, he
asked permission to relate an adventure of his own.
Anticipating assent, he moved forward his cushion,
and Genji opportunely awoke.

"At a time," began the Master of the Horse,
"when I was in a yet more humble position than that
which I now unworthily occupy, I loved a girl who
was such as I have described—not at all points admirable. For that excellent reason, coxcomb that I
was, I did not think of her as a life companion, but
considered my intercourse with her an agreeable
pastime, which I was free to vary by seeking similar
amusement elsewhere. She, however, was of a
fiercely jealous temper, which, in the circumstances,
I could not but regard as a serious blemish. Still,
she was so devoted to me, notwithstanding my poverty, that I forgave her everything. In time I became really attached to her, and then, instead of
mending my manners, I began to entertain the idea
that perhaps *she* might be cured of her jealousy.
Surely, thought I, devoted as she is, if I pretend to
grow cooler, she will take warning. I therefore be-
haved rather worse than usual, to which she objected

with more than her customary warmth. That gave me the opportunity that I had desired, and I read her a solemn lecture on the propriety of patience, and followed it up with a threat never again to see her if her jealous rages continued. On the other hand, if she would only act as I wished, as she would then be perfection itself, I could not think of straying from her. And, as my circumstances were likely to improve, we might be completely happy.

"To my surprise, this just and reasonable proposition, the result of much careful thought, she rejected with indignation. It was a small matter, she said, to put up with my mean condition; but to be obliged to wait from day to day for me to return to a sense of what was due to her was more than she could longer undertake to bear. Few words were best; if I did not at once reform, she would be driven to the conclusion that we had better part. This was so contrary to what I had expected and desired, that it threw me into a fit of anger. I had but wished to correct her one great failing, I declared, and, giving way to my emotions, I overwhelmed her with reproaches. The vixen responded by flying into a yet more violent passion; then, becoming quite beside herself, she suddenly seized my hand, and, before I could guess her intention, bit off a joint of my little finger."

A Rainy Night Entertainment

Needless to say, the unlucky Master of the Horse gave over his experiment. He left his too vivacious charmer, and, though he afterward made an unsuccessful attempt to reclaim her, he contrived, for a time, to find consolation with the one on whose account she had given way to such a regrettable fit of passion.

"My second flame," he continued, "was a poetess and a musician of talent, both gifts that I appreciate highly. Indeed, I may say she was no ordinary person. Still, she had her faults, and they were yet more serious than those of my first love. You shall judge. I had long been on excellent terms with her, and was becoming a little careless, when, one fine autumn evening, I happened to be driving out on a visit to a high official, and was joined on the way by a young nobleman of my acquaintance. The youth confided to me that he was in a hurry, for 'it would not do to keep a lady waiting.' The road skirted a park in which was her residence, and an ornamental lake that reflected the moonlight shone through the embrasures of the wall. The scene was one which might well awaken sentiment. I could not shut my heart against its seductions; I forgot my errand, dismounted, and entered the gateway. Within, in a sort of portico, my young friend was seated on a mat, rapt in a poetic reverie. His eyes were raised to the stars, his nostrils inhaled the rich perfume of the chrysanthemums in the garden, while a gentle breeze caused to flutter down about him the reddened leaves of the maples. I might have been miles away; he was unaware of my presence. I, for my part, was equally lost in amazement when, taking a flute from his bosom, he began to play the air of a love-song with which I had good reason to be familiar. He paused. In a moment the air was taken up from a distance with a soft strain upon the koto, so admirably played that there could be no room for doubt as to the performer.

"Quitting his seat, the youngster moved forward with an air of mingled timidity and assurance that, somehow, made me quite angry, stopping every now and then to pluck a flower, to repeat a stanza, or to gaze, like one entranced, upon the moon; while the unseen fair one exchanged the koto for a more seductive instrument, and played more passionate, more languorous melodies. At last he disappeared among the shadows of the garden, like a spirit in a dream. Well! He was in the right to be happy; she was an admirable musician. But though I, too, am a lover of the art, I derived little pleasure from it on that occasion. I can conceive that one might still keep up a flirtation with such a woman if she were one of those of the Court, whom we have seldom an opportunity to meet in private; but, even in that case, we should not regard her as approaching our ideal.

"Think, then," he continued, "how little reliance is to be placed in women. Either they are too jealous, or they themselves furnish grounds for jealous suspicions. Like lotus leaves floating before the wind, like dew on the lespedeza blossom, or hailstones among the bamboo grass, they delight us for a moment, but their charm disappears as soon as they are touched. The wisest course is to avoid them altogether. If you do not now believe me, you will when another seven years shall have passed over your heads. You will then know, perhaps but too well, that these romantic escapades of youth result in nothing but a damaged reputation."

Chiujio nodded, as one competent to bear witness to the justice of the speaker's remarks; and forgetting his usual caution, volunteered to support them with a story of his own. Nothing could have more delighted Genji, who had in vain essayed to draw him out. But he had not proceeded far before his feelings overpowered him, and he utterly broke down. In his case the lady had been neither jealous nor fickle; she had never bit his finger nor listened to another admirer. In fact, she had shown such unfailing patience with his irregularities that they had insensibly become such as he himself could not excuse.

At last she had sent him as a farewell gift a bunch of wild pinks, and had departed, leaving no clew by which he might hope to discover her. When he had sufficiently recovered himself, "Who, indeed, are we to select?" he sadly asked. "All this variety, all this perplexing difficulty of choice; and yet, it seems to be inevitable that, whatever choice we make, it turns out for the worse. Are we, then, to fix our thoughts upon some heavenly goddess? Alas! that, again, were only superstitious folly."

A general outburst of laughter greeted this last observation; and the Secretary was asked to relate something in his turn. He was loath to respond, and had to be spurred on by repeated solicitations; but, when he had finished—"Fie! What a devil of a woman," cried Genji; and, snapping their fingers, the company unanimously demanded "a better story." The Secretary, however, had no other to tell, and the conversation relapsed into generalities.

While the rain drummed upon the tiles and plashed in the broad gravelled spaces without, the trio of connoisseurs decided upon the accomplishments, the virtues, the beauties that they would require were they called upon to select from all creation the most perfect woman. She should have some learning, but not enough to be vain of. She should be gentle, but not too submissive. She should be able to turn a verse,

A Rainy Night Entertainment

but should not be constantly scribbling when more important matters claim her attention. Above all, she should never, like the Secretary's strong-minded sweetheart, assert a right to ignore the elementary rules of propriety. Genji, meanwhile, occupied himself in mentally picturing a fair creature in whom all these various attributes were happily united, and determined that, as soon as the special fast was over, he would begin to search for her in that middle class of poor gentlewomen, parvenues, and daughters of deputy-governors, of which his brother-in-law and the Master of the Horse had spoken, and with which so far he had had little or no acquaintance.

X

FURTHER ADVENTURES OF PRINCE GENJI

A FIRST search made Genji acquainted with a lady who repelled all his advances in such a way as to leave him no excuse for further pursuit. He endeavored to console himself with the reflection that he would out-live her husband, who was an old and ugly deputy-governor; but the man persisted in living, survived Genji's passion, and won his esteem. He was more, or, as it turned out, less fortunate in another quarter, and got in the way of driving out to the Rokujio suburb to visit a lady who had a magnificent residence there.

On one of these occasions it occurred to him that he had not for a long time seen his old nurse, who, he had been informed, had entered upon a life of re-ligious retirement in her son's house, in the vicinity. He therefore abandoned his projects for the even-ing, and turned in that direction. No one expecting him, the gate was closed, and it was some time before the key could be found. Meanwhile, Genji, looking about him from his carriage, saw behind the lattices of a neighboring dwelling some young women who

were evidently, on their side, observing him. The
house was of the poorer sort, but a white-flowered
convolvulus grew luxuriantly over the trellis, and
beautified the squalid place with its blossoms. Genji
hummed a verse of an old song :

> " Tell me, traveller,
> What flower is't that blossoms
> Beside you, yonder ? "

" Sir, it is the evening glory," replied one of his
attendants ; and Genji promptly sent the man to ask
for some. He returned with a fan on which was laid
a bunch of the white flowers ; and Koremitz, the
nurse's son, coming at the moment with the key, the
carriage was driven into the court-yard.

In conversation with his old nurse, Genji forgot
about the blossoms ; but, on taking leave, he remembered that he had noticed some writing on the fan
that had been sent with them, and, looking at it in
the lamplight, he found some verses in a delicate
handwriting traced on the white paper. The circumstance surprised him, for there was nothing to indi-
cate that the house was inhabited by people of refinement. It may well be, thought he, that here lives the
ideal fair one described by the Master of the Horse, and
he sent a suitable reply by Koremitz, whom he commissioned to find out all he could about his neighbors.

Koremitz was zealous, as much from a native love of intrigue as from a desire to please Genji. He soon discovered that a young lady, with a maid and a little girl, were staying at the house, and learned something of their history. He told Genji (but this was his own invention) that they were often visited by a gentleman; a general it appeared; and, in short, from one circumstance and another, he had established his identity, and it was no other but Chiujio. "What!" cried Genji, "the fellow has better luck than he deserves; for, plainly, he has found his runaway;" and his interest in the case was, as Koremitz intended it should be, greatly increased. He began, then, taking the most elaborate precautions against discovery (which greatly amused the sly Koremitz) to pay court to the lady, and soon thought he had reason to felicitate himself upon the progress he was making, never dreaming, all the while, that there was really no Chiujio in the way. He invariably delayed his visits until after dark, and came so carefully disguised that everybody about the place knew he was some great personage. But they humored his evident desire to remain incognito, being satisfied with Koremitz's assurances that he was a young gentleman of means and position who was not yet at liberty to choose for himself.

But the very fact that Chiujio never appeared to

trouble him, and that nobody spied upon him or asked him inconvenient questions, gave rise in Genji's mind to more extravagant fears of detection. There was no telling when he might run against his rival, who might create a scandal, or wait his time and take a sudden vengeance. Genji was, indeed, so careful to preserve appearances that, as our authoress remarks, " he can hardly be said to have accomplished anything downright marvellous : a fact which would have moved to scorn the heroes of earlier romances." He resolved, then, to remove Evening Glory, as he called her, to some place where they would be less open to observation.

It was late one night in August when he came to carry out this resolution. The moon shone through the cracks in the old paper screens that served for walls to the cottage. The neighboring farmers were already up, though it was yet long before dawn, and were talking to one another about the weather, the crops, and the markets on their way to work. From a distance came the noise of flails, and of the bleacher's mallet. The light foliage of a tuft of bamboos, in the space before the door, glistened with dew. A cricket was singing in some cranny, and, overhead, a flock of wild-geese was heard flying past.

These unwonted sights and sounds so impressed Genji, to whom life outside the palace walls was an unopened book, and the girl, in her cheap purple dress, looked so frail, and so much in harmony with her surroundings, that he thought it a pity to take her away. "Will she bear transplanting?" he asked himself. But she had consented to go with him, and he could not withdraw from the arrangement. The maid was to go with them.

They were getting into the carriage, when an old man in a neighboring hut began to pray aloud. "What can he be praying for?" asked Genji; "his day will soon be over." "O! Divine Guide of the Future," muttered the old fellow, invoking Buddha; and it seemed like a reply to his question. Genji fell into a reverie on the limitless round of existences that lies before us; but the incident appeared to give rise to serious reflections on the part of his fair companion also, and, rousing himself, he pressed her to exchange vows of eternal love and fidelity. She, however, could not be stimulated to cheerfulness, and would give no promise.

They were not far on their way when the moon set in a fog which had risen from the rice fields and hid the embankment along which they were travelling. The carriage blinds had been drawn up, and their sleeves were wet with the mist. Genji began to feel depressed; and the girl was sunk in melancholy. He plied her with questions as to her past, which did not tend to raise her spirits, but the contrary. The only answer he could gain was a verse of an old ballad, which she repeated in a low tone:

> " Like the lonely moon
> I wander o'er the mountains;
> Whether true or false
> My love be, now, I know not,
> For clouds have come between us."

It was the first time she had alluded (so Genji imagined) to Chiujio; and he pressed her no further.

The steward, who was in charge of the house that Genji had selected, had received no notice of their coming. The few domestics were asleep, and they could get nothing but rice gruel for breakfast. The place was encircled by gloomy pine woods; the garden had been suffered to grow wild, and the pond was filled with weeds. The day wore away. Toward evening the air became oppressively still. Genji, more than ever distracted, thought, " Now the Emperor is asking for me; now the Lady of Rokujio is expecting me; could she know where I am and in what company, how furious she would be ! " He grew more and more restless and apprehensive, and the girl remained "sad as the weed in the creek."

Night came on, and Genji fell asleep to dream of the jealous woman of Rokujio, threatening and up-

braiding him. He awoke in a tremor, with a feeling
that some one had actually entered the room. He
drew his sword, and called the maid. Her mistress's
sleep appeared to be disturbed, she said : she was
often troubled with nightmare. Genji aroused two
of his men, one of whom went to procure a light,
while the other paced through the corridors, twang-
ing his bowstring and shouting " Look out for fire ! "
to scare off the demon.

Meanwhile the poor girl had grown rapidly worse,
and, at last, had sunk into unconsciousness. Genji,
to whom this experience was totally new, could think
of nothing but foxes and demons, and wished that a
priest were by to exorcise them. He sent for Koremitz and his brother, who was in orders ; but
neither came. Suddenly the girl grew rigid ; and,
at the same moment, the figure of the Lady of Rokujio, that he had seen in his dream, passed before his
eyes. "Oh ! " he cried, "this is like the wicked
phantoms in old tales ! " He took the girl's hand
and called to her. She was dead.

Neither Koremitz nor his brother had yet appeared.
The maid, Ukon, had fallen upon the mats, crying ;
and Genji began to fear that the mysterious apparition
might claim her, also, as a victim. The night was
stormy. The wind sighed among the pines and made
the lamp flicker ; and he fancied that the sliding

screens that formed the walls of the room opened and
closed of themselves to admit ghostly visitors. He
was sure that the apparition which he had seen was
the revengeful double of his other mistress. This
sort of phantom, he had been told, could leave the
sleeping body to which it belonged, and put in action
malicious thoughts of which the owner was scarcely
conscious.

Day, at last, dawned, and Koremitz arrived, but
without the priest, who had returned to his monastery. The man was as young as his master, and as
new to such a situation. Between them, they could
contrive no better than to take the corpse, while it
was yet dusk, and without awaking the steward or
his family, to a convent in the mountain close by,
where the nuns were accustomed to receive the dead,
and where Koremitz had an acquaintance upon
whom he could rely. This Koremitz undertook to
do by himself, making use of Genji's carriage; he
packed his master off home, where the latter denied
himself to all comers on the plea that he had become
"unclean" by unwittingly passing too near a dead
body.

The next day he could not be restrained from
proceeding to the convent. Koremitz guided him
there, by an unfrequented path, after nightfall.
They forded the river Kamo, passed the lonely grave-

yard of Toribeno, and approached the convent, which was perched on a steep eminence at a considerable height above the plain. A few lights shone dimly through the paper walls, which made the place look like a huge lantern lost amid the trees and rocks. The services were over in the neighboring temples, and in the deep stillness they could hear distinctly each word of the prayers for the dead which a female voice was repeating.

It was Ukon who was reading beside the body with her back to the lamp. From her Genji learned the facts of Evening Glory's short existence. She was daughter of a general who had squandered his fortune in trying to advance his ambition. After his death she had fallen in with Chiujio; but the threats which his family had secretly conveyed to her alarmed her so that she had concealed herself from him where Genji had found her. So much Koremitz had been told; he added that Chiujio had re-discovered her in order to inflame Genji's curiosity and incite him to rivalry. Genji's carriage had been mistaken for Chiujio's by the maid; hence the present of flowers. She had never varied in her affections, and had regarded Genji only as a friend and protector. Her reticence had been due to his own absurd precautions; he had not seen fit to discover himself, and she but imitated his reserve.

Further Adventures of Prince Genji

There was about this time at Court a lively maiden named Tayu, who was aware of Genji's liking for extraordinary acquaintances, and who had a friend, poor, proud, ugly, timid, and unprotected, to whom the prince's favor, could she gain it for her, might prove a beginning of good fortune. Tayu, as clever as she was disinterested, readily excited Genji's curiosity by telling him of the Princess Hitachi's modest bearing, her skill in music and other accomplishments, and her beauty, which appeared all the brighter from its contrast with her sad condition. She dwelt alone in an old mansion fast falling into decay, in the midst of grounds once beautiful, now wild enough to be the abode of a wood devil. Newly enriched ex-governors, anxious to cut a figure at the capital, had made her excellent offers for the estate, but her pride would not suffer her to part with it. Neither would she sell her ancient furniture, much of which was so old as to be valuable from its rarity. She despised as lowborn upstarts the fashionable people who tried to induce her to sell them her treasures. Her only visitor was her brother, an eccentric old priest, as poor and proud as herself; and the two would beguile the time together by reading over the old treatises, the ancient romances, and poems with which her mouldering book-shelves were stocked.

Here was a romantic case, indeed! What more could a professed seeker of adventures desire? But the termination of the affair with Evening Glory was still too fresh in Genji's mind for him to be easily led into a new scrape of the sort.

The artful Tayu, however, was not discouraged. She kept on sounding her friend's praises at every opportunity, and when, at length, Genji expressed a desire to see the princess, began to throw difficulties in the way; but when he seemed willing to drop the matter, she spurred him on with fresh inducements. She had quite as much trouble with her princess, whose consciousness of her own awkward manners and want of even ordinary attractions, made her a peculiarly difficult subject to manage. When, at last, the two were brought together, Tayu contrived that her friend's shortcomings should not be too obvious. Still, it was long before she could prevail upon Genji to go a second time. One evening, after she had been teasing him to no purpose, the fancy seized him to make a call alone. Snow had begun to fall, and the foolish princess, with no Tayu to guide her, stepped out upon the balcony to watch it. Genji followed, and had a good opportunity to notice the defects of figure, face, and carriage which Tayu, on their first meeting, had skilfully concealed. She was, indeed, the type of those meagre princesses of

Further Adventures of Prince Genji

Japanese popular art, whose long, expressionless faces are ornamented with noses of startling proportions tinged at the extremity with pink. Genji mentally compared this feature to the trunk of the elephant of Fugen, * which, the holy books say, is like a red lily. Her movements were stiff and constrained, and her tall and languid figure seemed scarcely able to bear the weight of her old-fashioned garments of silk and sable. "But why be so critical?" thought he, "and why not rather seek out her good points? She is not without them. It cannot be denied, for instance, that her modesty is so great as to be almost embarrassing." His resentment at the trick that had been played upon him gave way to pity. "You are a lucky girl," he soliloquized on his departure, "for, if I were like other people, I should have little sympathy for you;" and he determined to send her, at once, workmen to put the place in repair, brocade for dresses, and some rolls of cloth for her servants. "I must see to it also," thought he, "that an allowance is made to her by the Emperor. There are many less deserving recipients of his bounty."

In this mood, a wild orange-tree near the broken gate, which the starved porter had some difficulty in opening, caught his eye. It was laden with the snow that had fallen heavily during his stay, and the frail

*Samatabhadra, a disciple of Buddha.

branches threatened to break beneath the weight. He ordered one of his men to shake it off. The motion communicated itself to the branches of a pine-tree that was standing by, and from them also the snow slid off "like a wave." To the apt reader, the incident conveys a moral. Genji's kindness to the ugly princess which was " as the reflection of the starry heavens in a bowl of water," had relieved him in like manner of the load of remorse that he had in-curred by his thoughtless dealings with Chiujio's sweetheart, and showed him in some degree worthy of the supreme good fortune that was in store for him.

When Tayu took him in hand, he was but just recovered from a severe illness brought on by his exposure to the night-air on the occasion of his visit to the convent. To complete his cure, a famous hermit of Mount Kurama, who was said to be more successful than others in casting out the evil spirits that cause disease, was sent for. But he excused himself on the score of his great age, being now too old and feeble to travel to Kioto. The prince, there-fore, went to the hermit, and, out of regard for the holy man's reputation, which might suffer if he failed to effect a cure, he took but a few attendants with him, and set out as privately as possible. Up to this time, Genji had never been so far from the city, and the mountain scenery was a revelation to him.

Further Adventures of Prince Genji

The cherry-trees were still in bloom, though it was past their flowering season in the capital. They found the saint in his cave ; he received them warmly, and gave his patient a talismanic prescription to swallow. That done, Genji enjoyed the view from the terrace before the cave, while the hermit proceeded with his exorcisms.

The scene included a great part of the plain as well as a distant view of the city, but Genji was most attracted by a pretty cottage on the side of the mountain, a little below where he stood. It was surrounded by a picturesque garden in which a lady and a little girl were taking the air. After spending the day in prayer, the hermit desired him to stay that night at the temple, close by, and be further prayed for. To this Genji assented, but the evening was long, and the conversation of the good monks was tedious ; so, making some excuse, he stole out again, and, under cover of the increasing darkness, took a nearer view of the cottage and its garden. A room at the western end of the house was open to the air, and before an image of Buddha a nun was reading aloud the evening service. Though apparently only about forty years of age, her voice trembled, and she looked like one at the point of death. The child that Genji had already noticed ran in and out, and the nun occasionally interrupted her devotions to speak to her. From what he overheard of their talk Genji gathered that the nun was anxious about the little one's future. The master of the house who was a priest attached to the temple, came in to announce that he had just heard of the prince's arrival, and was about to pay his respects to him ; so Genji, determining that the interview should not end without his securing an invitation, returned as quickly as possible to the monastery.

The priest was proud to conduct him back again, and to show him all the windings of a little stream that ran through his garden, now lit up with lanterns. The good man talked by the way so eloquently of great things and little, that he touched his hearer's heart. "How much better it were to live simply and calmly like this priest, than as I have been living," said Genji to himself; "especially if I had such a pretty girl as I have seen this evening to educate." He had unconsciously hit upon the only way in which he might secure his ideal.

The priest gave him some account of the little one's parentage, and of the reasons that had led his sister, the nun, to take charge of her. In brief, her mother was dead, and her father, a prominent man at Court, was both unfit and disinclined to care for her properly. Remembering the nun's feeble condition, Genji thought he might possibly gain possession of the child, and sounded her guardians on the matter; but they politely declined his offers of protection. He felt, however, that it would be wrong to permit her father to assume authority over her. The nun dying, some weeks later, he secretly carried her away. In the young Violet, as her character unfolded itself, Genji found united all the qualities that he had admired, or the lack of which he had regretted in so many others. In short, she grew to be the ideal woman pronounced undiscoverable by the philosophers, his friends. As the name of this paragon is the same as the author's,* some cynical commentators have supposed that in Genji's Violet she has presented us with a picture of her own perfections.

Murasaki does not quit her hero at this point in his career. The great length of her romance was, doubtless, one of its chief recommendations in an age of few books. She follows Genji in his voluntary exile at Suma, made necessary by many indiscretions, of which his abduction of the young Violet was the least; and in his triumphant return when, his first wife having died, he married her; and all through his later life of ambition and public usefulness. His character, as she draws it, is consistently inconsistent. Genji is clever, but vacillating; patient in misfortune, but reckless in prosperity; generous to his

* Murasaki = Violet.

friends and bearing no malice against his enemies, yet unjust at times to both alike; open to high influences, yet more often ruled by others of an unworthy nature. This fidelity to real life is shown also in her sketches of other characters, in the pious old gentleman at Akashi, who so long rejected all offers of marriage for his daughter that it was supposed he expected some god to take pity on her, and in the cold and haughty lady Hollyhock, and the vindictive lady of Rokujio quarrelling over places from which to view a court procession. It is what gives her work its lasting value, and will yet, perhaps, gain her a place among the world's greatest female writers.

XI

HORRIFIC EXPLOITS OF YORIMITSU

A POPULAR tale, as distinct from myth and from literary fiction, cannot arise until there is a populace. Japan does not appear to have produced anything of the sort until the cultivated society of the Court had become widely separated from the mass of settled and more or less intelligent citizens. At Nara the entire population seems to have held practically the same beliefs, prejudices, and opinions, to have been animated by the same sentiments, and possessed of the same tastes. As yet, citizen and courtier were almost convertible terms, and no general fusion of the dominant race with the aborigines had occurred. In the literature of Kioto we find for the first time frequent references to class distinctions, and expressions of surprise at any appearance of refinement in the lower grades of society. But by the end of the tenth century the people had begun to form a literature of their own, which continued slowly to develop as that of the Court sank into decay. A few of the earlier folk-tales have survived, loaded with many additions,

but unchanged in essence. The most celebrated of
these has for its hero Yorimitsu of the Minamoto, a
descendant of Genji and contemporary of Madame
Murasaki. It exhibits a vulgar ideal whose elements
are derived, indeed, from the more grewsome of the
ancient myths, from Buddhist legends, and the more
artistic fictions that amused the Court, but which on
the whole differs greatly from anything that appears
in them. There is in it no effort to make fable sub-
serve a serious purpose; no ironical criticism of current beliefs and assumptions. The story is told for
pure delight in the grotesque. The hero is known
to have been employed by the Emperor Murakami, in
A.D. 947, to exterminate a powerful band of brigands
who had their headquarters in the wooded and mountainous province of Tamba, not far from the capital.
On this fact the principal legend connected with him
is founded. But like many of our heroes of chivalry,
Yorimitsu is but a shadowy figure, who generally
remains in the background while one or other of
his four squires performs deeds of desperate valor in
the foreground. Each of these is, or has been, the
centre of a group of legends; and we hear of Kintoki
as a boy in the forest of Ashigara amusing himself by
pulling a fat bear about by the tail; and of Tsuna how
he once delivered his chief out of the toils of a demon
spider. Of Suyetada and Sadamichi we hear com-

Horrific Exploits of Yorimitsu

paratively little. Tsuna has evidently been the favor-. ite with the story-tellers, and has succeeded to most of the tales invented for the others. The legend of the spider betrays a singular and refined taste in the horrific that would charm a *fin-de-siècle* story-teller.

It happened on a day that master and man—Yorimitsu and Tsuna—were riding across the moor of Rendai, thinking, belike, of nothing, when they suddenly became aware of a small white cloud floating in the azure sky above them. Now, it is nothing uncommon to see a single cloud in a clear summer sky ; but this one had features that might well attract the notice of a knight-errant and his squire out of a job. Two shadowy cavities, like empty eye-sockets, opened below its domed and glistening summit. Two other openings appeared close together beneath, and under these depended a fringe of shining cloudlets that looked exactly like a row of teeth. In short, it was as well-shaped a death's head as was ever carved in ivory or drawn upon a Buddhist scroll. To go where glory led them was the sole aim in life of our two heroes. They lost not a moment in changing their course and following the promising token. Toward evening it brought them to a ruined habitation, surrounded by many leagues of moor and fen, and above the lonely house it melted out in air. Tsuna knocked. In answer to his summons, there hobbled out an old,

old woman—so old that she was obliged to prop her
drooping eyelid with her staff to take a look at them,
and then to support her pendant lip in the same fashion ere she could mumble forth a welcome. But,
though it was with the utmost difficulty that she
spoke, the old lady hardly needed an invitation to tell
her tale.

"Here, in this house," she said, "I have served
five generations of a great family long since extinct.
Oh! I have seen many changes in my time, and this
was once a resplendent mansion, where heroes like
yourselves were sure of a hospitable welcome. Now,
for these many years, no one has come this way but
demons, who make the ruin their half-way house in
their nightly journeys across the waste. I doubt not
that some god has sent the token that you have followed, in order that ye, brave gentlemen, may rid the
world of the monsters that have depopulated the district, and enable this poor old woman to end her days
in peace."

Yorimitsu, on hearing this, instantly dismounted.
Tsuna had already done so. Demons were their
game; so they hobbled their horses at some distance,
and let the old woman lead them to the kitchen, the
only room that was in tolerable repair. Here they
took up their quarters for the night, and awaited what
fate might send them in the way of an adventure.

Horrific Exploits of Yorimitsu

Scarcely had they made themselves comfortable when night came suddenly with a storm of wind and rain ; and soon, to the distant drumming of the thunder, they heard as it were the tramping of a countless army marching through the dark. A goblin army: battalions of reanimated corpses ; brigades of skeletons ; legions of murdered men. All night it defiled before the ruin to the music of the storm ; but the Knight and Squire kept their post undaunted.

The thing had grown monotonous, and they had begun to consider the chances of a sortie, when toward morning, a spirit left the ranks and came toward them. It was attired like a nun, but its diminutive body carried a head of enormous size, and two long, white, thread-like arms. Yorimitsu and Tsuna put themselves in a posture of defence, but the goblin only laughed at them and vanished. At the same time, the rearguard of the demon army swept by ; the storm was dying out in the distance ; and our two adventurers, believing their trial over, prepared for sleep.

But now appeared another spectre, not a bit repulsive or alarming ; beautiful, on the contrary, as a dream. A dream it, in fact, appeared to both of them, especially to Yorimitsu, whose eyes closed upon the delightful vision as it floated softly toward them. But the prudent Tsuna, though sorely tempted to follow his example, roused himself, and saw, out of the

corner of an eye, the lovely apparition transform itself into a huge spider, which proceeded with un-
imaginable celerity to weave a web of steel about his
sleeping master. One does not, when confronted
with such a sight, ask one's self or others what it may
possibly mean; Tsuna whipped out his sword and
hacked away at the meshes. Yorimitsu awoke, and
with a lucky blow, wounded the monster. It disappeared, but left a trail of white blood behind it, following which across the threshold and out into the
moor, they came to the creature's den, where it
writhed its jointed legs convulsively over a heap of
human bones; and, even while they looked, from a
tremendous wound in the abdomen, the work of
Yorimitsu's sabre, there rolled out a ghastly mass of
skulls. Then the cocks crew in farms far away, the
sun rose, and our two heroes sought the ancient dame
to bid her farewell. She was nowhere to be found,
however, and with dark surmises that she might have
been herself the goblin, the two resumed their journey.

It was the same Tsuna who, according to the story-
tellers and the blind shampooers, had the fight with
the ogre at the gate called Rashōmon, in Kioto, which
cut out work for all the four squires and their chief,
and led to the greatest of their exploits.

In the province of Omi, which runs as a border

Horrific Exploits of Yorimitsu

about Lake Biwa, there had lived a very handsome
but dissipated fellow whose robberies and misdeeds
of all sorts grew to be intolerable, so that his father-
in-law was forced to put an end to him. He left a son,
who, as soon as he was able to crawl, began where
his worthy father had left off. He manifested, while
still an infant, a tremendous capacity for drinking
saké, and displayed thereafter such a villainous spirit
that his mother took him, at seven years old, and lost
him in the forest of Higashi. The youngster made
himself quite at home there, and did not lack for
nurses. The tengu, wild creatures with beak - like
noses, dwelling in nests, and provided with wings and
claws, were delighted to take charge of him ; and he
daily grew in strength and villainy to the admiration
of all the ogres, wood-spirits, and outlaws lurking in
the wilderness. Admitted to their society, he became
in a short time their leader, plundering the villages
all about, and terrorizing the country. Driven from
mountain to mountain by the guardian gods, the band
at length settled for a while at Nishigata near Kioto.
But, unluckily for them, Saint Kobo Daishi, then
just returned from his studies in China, had been
commissioned by the Empress to build his monastery
there.* The ogres at first attempted to oppose him.
They caused big trees to spring up over night in the

* This is an anachronism, as Kobo Daishi died in 834.

ground that he had cleared during the day. But the holy man prayed to Buddha, and the trees vanished. Forced to migrate once more, the band retired to the mountains of Tamba, where they fortified the approaches to their cave and recommenced their depredations.

By degrees they grew so bold as to enter by night the streets of the Imperial City, and carry off young women and rob belated pedestrians. None knew how they gained admittance. The guards appeared to be vigilant, and every measure was taken for security; but the brigands continued their attacks, and the people became afraid to leave their houses after nightfall. So matters stood when Yorimitsu came to pay his respects to the new Emperor. His four squires accompanied him as usual, and Tsuna, hearing of the doings of the ogres, determined in his heart that he would have a brush with them. So he asked and obtained permission to keep watch at the south gate, the farthest from the palace, near which most of the crimes that had so alarmed the citizens had been committed. At the usual hour for changing watch he took up his post in the guard-house. Nothing happened until about midnight, when he was aware of a strange drowsiness stealing over him. As it grew upon him the wind blew up furiously, and, nine parts asleep, he felt himself being lifted bodily into the air by the top-knot. Notwithstanding, the drowsy feeling gained on him so that he had great difficulty in shaking it off. Making a supreme effort, he succeeded in drawing his long sword, and striking blindly, he was so fortunate as to lop off his captor's arm clean from the shoulder. He and the arm fell to the ground together. The ogre fled howling through the storm, and, for that night, Kioto slept in peace.

Following the advice of a wise old priest, well versed in demonology, Tsuna enclosed the frightful trophy in a stone coffer securely locked, while for seven days and seven nights he propitiated the gods, to whom the ogre might be related, by fasting and prayer, in strict silence and seclusion. He had almost accomplished his penance when, on the seventh night, there came a knocking at the door. "Who is it?" cried Tsuna. "It is your poor old mother," replied a voice without. "I have heard of your fine deed of arms, and have come to congratulate you. Pray let me in." Tsuna explained the necessity he was under of finishing his vigil in silence and alone; but the old mother continued her entreaties. He could not find it in his heart to turn her away after her long journey.

Soon as admitted, however, she began to show herself extremely curious about the arm in the box.

" Was it real? Was it actually there? " She had often heard of such matters, but, old woman as she was, she had never seen nor touched an ogre's arm. Would not her brave son accord her the pleasure to examine such a rare curiosity?

Tsuna yielded. He rashly opened the chest, and delivered the monstrous arm into the bony hand stretched out for it. As he did so he remarked, what he had not noticed before, that his mother was one-handed. But he had no time to ask for an explanation. The old woman, who was really no other than the ogre, started up, and cleverly fitting the arm-bone into its socket, laughed loudly, and flew out in an eddy of wind by the smoke-hole.

Who then was crestfallen but our brave Tsuna? He reported the untoward occurrence to Yorimitsu, who reported it to the Mikado, who ordered Yorimitsu to lead at once an expedition against the ogres, and exterminate them. It was easy talking; but Yorimitsu knew that if he set out with a large following, the band would not fail to hear of his mission and would decamp. Strategy was requisite in dealing with the monsters. So, taking only his four lieutenants, he disguised himself and them as Buddhist pilgrims, and, leaving the Rashōmon gate early in the morning, without making known his errand to any one, he struck out for the land of Tamba. Each man car-

Horrific Exploits of Yorimitsu

ried in addition to his staff and bell, a bamboo bucket full of saké, and instead of the priest's pack of holy books, his arms stowed away in a knapsack.

They wandered for some days in the mountains without finding any trace of the robbers. They were beginning to think of abandoning the enterprise when they were joined by a well-disposed forest god in the guise of a woodcutter, who, ashamed probably of the uncivil doings of his wilder relatives, guided them as far as to the foot of Oeyama, where the band had established their fortress. There, they presently discovered a young woman washing some bloodied raiment in a stream. She was thrall to the ogres, and, after much persuasion she led them to their cavern.

Now, the demons know that priests belong in a measure to the supernatural world, like themselves; and, as these priests made no preparations to begin a spiritual warfare against them, but, on the contrary, offered to share with them the contents of their saké buckets, they were amicably received. Priests and ogres held a grand carouse until the buckets were emptied; and then commenced an earth-shaking ballet. Tengu and horned demons, priests and outlaws, black robe and hairy mantle, flew round and about the cavern. The young woman that the brigands had stolen furnished the music.

The fun was at its height, when Tsuna, engaging in

a friendly wrestling match with the chief ogre, caught his hands and held them, laughing, while Yorimitsu, who unperceived had got out his weapon, with a sweeping stroke severed the wretch's head from his neck, so neatly that the couple danced on again for some seconds, the ogre with his head still in place, and no whit aware of what had happened.

While the attention of the company was directed to Tsuna and his partner, the other companions of Yorimitsu had had time to exchange their priests' gowns for armor, and to draw their weapons. And now befel a slaughter great and memorable. The five champions rushed upon the demons, who, though numerous, were in poor condition for fighting, as they had drunk the greater portion of the saké. Here, an ogre's head shot up to the ceiling on a jet of blood, and fell with gnashing teeth on Yorimitsu's helmet. There, lay others of the band cut and carved in every style. Not one escaped. The robbers who had been left on guard by the stockade, ran in to aid their comrades. Their throats were cut, ribs pierced, heads broken as they came. Last, the victorious knights cut down the two guards of the charnel house, who had not stirred from their posts. The robbers' fastness was set on fire, and, lighted by its flames, and taking with them the rescued captives laden with booty, they returned triumphantly to Kioto.

Horrific Exploits of Yorimitsu

Such is the legend ; but now for the truth of history !

Beside the bare fact of his expedition against the robbers of Tamba, about the only thing known with certainty concerning Yorimitsu is that he died in his bed, at a good old age, in A.D. 1021.

XII

FORTUNES OF THE GEN

By the beginning of the twelfth century the two great military families had completely tranquillized the country, and a short period of unexampled prosperity succeeded. The Taira, the descendants of the Emperor Uda's favorite, Takamochi, had cleared the Inland Sea of pirates, and had restored order among the turbulent southern clans, while their rivals of the Gen, or Minamoto, completed the conquest of northern Japan. The five Home Provinces, Yamashiro, Yamato, Kawachi. Izumi, and Settsu, had long enjoyed the most profound peace. Whatever the faults of the Court, the country under its immediate protection was, as a rule, well governed and lightly taxed. In times of dearth taxes were wholly remitted, and we read how, on one such occasion, the Emperor took up his residence in a countryman's grass hut to set an example of economy to his subordinates. In more prosperous seasons, the happy peasants might be seen trotting into Kioto with their tribute of rice, or silk, or yarn, bells jingling at their horses' tails, and themselves arrayed in holiday attire.

But the time was already at hand when this Utopian state of things was to give way for over four centuries to ever-increasing disorder. It was no longer against Aino savages, "grass rebels;" * or hunted outlaws that the warrior had to fight, but against men of his own race and condition, often of his own sept. The control of the Court was to be the prize of contention, and the Home Provinces the most frequent scene of warfare.

Excepting a few battle hymns in the "Kojiki," the Japanese have no war-songs, properly so called ; but the following idyls may bring before the reader, more clearly than would pages of description, the nature of the feudal contests that so long distressed the country. The sentiment of profound melancholy that appears in the first is more touching than anything in the earlier literature. It reveals the growth of the feudal spirit, and brings us so far nearer to modern feelings and ideas. The warder complains at being left behind in garrison when his chief departs on a distant and dangerous expedition. He thinks of the coming winter, when the snow will block the mountain-passes and cut off communication

* So called because they hid in the long grass with which the moors are covered in summer.

between the castle and the force in the field. The allusion in the first stanza is to the Sacred Virgin, always a princess of the Imperial house, sent from Kioto to the temple of Yamada, in Ise, accompanied by a splendid retinue, on the accession of a new Mikado. It appears that she went most of the way by sea.

WAR IN AUTUMN.

Saw'st thou Ise's maid
O'er stormy seas, to exile
　　Carried, sick at heart?
As sad the tints of Autumn
Through drifts of rain appearing.

Bitter is the time
That friend from old friend severs,
　　Forced to dwell apart,
Nor one the other aiding;

Bitter is the day
That sends the loved guest homeward;
　　But, of all days worst,
That when the faithful clansman
　　Sees his lord march forth.

Long, long the empty spaces
　　Wistfully he scans;
For ring of armor listening,
Hears but the wild duck calling.

" War in Spring " describes the joy of the farmer at the prospect that the scene of war is to be re-

moved to other fields, and that he will be permitted
to reap the crop that he has sown. We must
imagine that the bowmen and spearmen of Yoshitsune's army have just marched by along the muddy
roads, under the rain-filled blossoms, in hot pursuit
of the enemy.

WAR IN SPRING.

Sowing wide the rain,
The soft gray clouds foregather
In the chilly air ;
And weeps the ice-clad willow
Into the misty river.

Minamoto's lord
Kawadzura's routed forces
Drives through Yoshino ;
And, now, our heart rejoices
In the growing Spring.
Up on the mountain ridges,
Down the hollow glens,
A host of blossoms greets him.
Every wind that blows
Wafts far and wide their fragrance
And Yoshitsune's fame.

Of prose narratives of the wars there is an abundance. The *Heike Monogatari*, or "Story of the
Heike" (Taira), and the *Hogen Monogatari*, or
"Story of the Gen," are the principal sources for
the historian who would treat of the first period of

the civil wars, that of the contest between these two great families.

Among the causes that led to the outbreak was the predominance in civil affairs of the Fujiwara. Claiming to be as ancient as the Imperial house, that family had long monopolized all the important civil offices throughout the Empire, leaving the military control to the Minamoto in the north, and the Taira in the south. But after the complete pacification of the Empire, the chiefs of both the military clans came to reside in Kioto. Each was accompanied by a large following, and, their former occupation gone, they continually encroached on the privileges of the Fujiwara. The latter had developed the astute policy of inducing each successive Emperor to resign and enter a monastery after a reign of a few years. The occupant of the throne was seldom more than a mere youth, often a child, and, though theoretically his will was law, he was completely under the control of his guardians and advisers, who were nearly all selected from the different branches of the Fujiwara. The Emperor Shirakawa, who ascended the throne at the age of twenty-one, was forced to retire at thirty-five, in favor of his son, Horikawa, who was made Emperor at the mature age of nine. Horikawa was followed by Toba, who began to reign at six, and abdicated at sixteen.

Shiutoku succeeded him at four years old and retired at twenty-four, to be succeeded by Konoye,
also four years old, who died at seventeen. Konoye
adopted as his heir his elder brother, Go-Shirakawa,
thus threatening the dominant position of the Fujiwara. The latter, aided by part of the Minamoto,
endeavored to enthrone the lineal heir in disregard
of the late Emperor's wishes; but the Taira espoused
the cause of Go-Shirakawa, and, defeating their
enemies in a pitched battle, seated him upon the
throne. Thus began the long feud between the clans.

But the new Emperor was allowed to wield no
more actual authority than his predecessors. Kiyomori, the head of the Taira, following the tactics of
the deposed Fujiwara, usurped all the powers of the
government. Go-Shirakawa reigned but three years,
when he, also, was packed off to a monastery. Another succession of child Emperors followed. Nijo,
aged at his accession eighteen, died at twenty-four;
Rokujo, proclaimed Emperor when scarcely one year
old, was deposed at four, and, after an interregnum,
was succeeded by Takakura, aged eight, who abdicated at twenty-one. Antoku, the last of the puppet
Emperors under the Taira, began to reign at three
and was drowned at the sea fight of Dan-No-Ura,
which brought the Taira usurpation to an end.

His power established, Kiyomori treated the conquered with such excessive severity, that even those of the Minamoto who had fought on his side were driven to conspire against him. Their plans were not allowed to ripen. The Taira set upon them in the streets of Kioto, and slaughtered them almost to a man. The Minamoto chieftain, Yoshitomo, fled to Owari, where he was assassinated. Kiyomori again snowed the heavy hand of the novice in his measures against the remnant of the clan, and filled most of the Court offices with members of his family. His daughter became the consort of the Emperor Takakura. His relations were appointed to rule over thirty provinces. But he lived to see his work almost completely undone, and the fallen fortunes of his rivals restored as by magic.

In the rout of the Minamoto one of the young sons of the vanquished chieftain, Yoritomo, became separated from the rest of the family. He was discovered by a captain of the Taira and brought to Kioto, but was saved by the intercession of Kiyomori's mother. The man who had found him, one Hōjō Tokimasa, was permitted to rear and educate the boy, and was held responsible for his conduct. Tokimasa retired with his ward to his own fief at Idzu. There Yoritomo fell in love with the pretty daughter of his captor, Masago. But he was a politic young man, and, knowing that her father intended Masago for a prominent noble of his own clan, he deemed it prudent to transfer his affections to her older sister. His letters, however, were delivered by his servant to the younger, and chance and inclination together determined Yoritomo upon risking an elopement with her. Masago had a strong hold upon her father's affections, and she quickly obtained forgiveness for herself and her husband. More than that, she brought Hōjō over to the cause of the Minamoto. Together with Yoritomo, he entered into correspondence with the scattered survivors of the clan, of which his son-in-law was now the head, and with the ex-Emperor Go-Shirakawa, who had been sent into exile by Kiyomori.

A rendezvous was appointed in the Hakone Mountains, but only a few hundred men answered the summons. They were attacked by the Taira and easily defeated. Yoritomo and a few of his adherents took refuge the night after the battle in a hollow tree. He was again saved by an enemy, who, being sent to search the tree, pronounced it empty. A wood pigeon which had its nest in its branches, and which had not been disturbed by the fugitives, flew off at the approach of the searching party, and the leader took that for sufficient proof that no one had preceded them. A few days later Yoritomo was again in imminent danger of capture, and would have been taken, had not a priest hidden him in his closet. At last he got away by sea to the peninsula of Awa, where he gathered a small band, and, returning to the mainland, again took the field in the very scene of his defeat.

Among the first to enter into Yoritomo's plans had been his younger half-brother, Yoshi-Tsune. Son of the murdered Yoshitomo by his mistress, a peasant girl of extraordinary beauty, the tyrant at Kioto had spared his life for her sake. Kiyomori thought to put him out of the way by sending him to the monastery of Kuramayama, near Kioto, to be educated as a priest. But the "Young Ox," as the monks nick-named him because of his strength and insubordination, refused to join their order. He escaped, and, in the company of a pedlar, made his way to the province of Mutsu, in the extreme north of Japan, where the governor, a Fujiwara, received him into his service. He now came forward to Yoritomo's aid with what following he could muster among the many enemies that Kiyomori's grasping policy had made for him in the northern provinces. Yoritomo, so reinforced, found himself at the head of a considerable army. Taught prudence by his recent reverses, he intrenched himself at Kamakura, not far from the site of the present capital, Tokio; and having now a secure base of operations, made ready for a forward movement on Kioto. In the midst of these preparations, Kiyomori died, beseeching his son and successor to waste no time in funeral ceremonies, but lay the head of Yoritomo of the Minamoto on his tomb.

At the opening of the campaign, the younger of the two brothers, Yoshitsune, was in command at Kamakura; Yoritomo had returned to his old recruiting ground at Awa, east of the bay of Tokio; and his cousin, Yoshinaka, was posted with a large band in the mountains of Shinano, between Kamakura and the capital. At the news of Kiyomori's death, Yoshinaka, without waiting for orders or reinforcements, marched at once on Kioto. In a pitched battle outside the city he defeated the much larger army sent against him, and entered the capital in triumph. Kiyomori's son, Munemori, the young emperor, Antoku, and most of the Court escaped, and Yoshinaka, construing this retreat to be equivalent to an abdication, put Antoku's brother, Go-Toba, then seven years old, upon the throne. His easy success turned Yoshinaka's head. He arrogated to himself the title of shogun (commander in chief), assumed to be the power behind the throne, and prepared to put down his cousins, Yoshitsune and Yoritomo. The former was therefore sent from Kamakura against him, Yoritomo occupying the stronghold with his new levies. Yoshinaka moved out to Fushimi, a marshy place on the banks of the Yodogawa, a little south of Kioto, to engage Yoshitsune's army. He was defeated; and in flying from the battle-field, his horse becoming mired in a rice swamp, he was shot in the forehead with an arrow.

Yoshitsune was now master of the situation. He did not rest upon his laurels. He turned his arms against the Taira that still held out at Fukuwara, near Kobe, to which place Kiyomori had at one time removed the capital. The place was carried by assault. Munemori, who commanded, fled to the castle of Yashima, which Yoshitsune also took and burned. Munemori then joined his partisans of the Court in Shikoku, but, fearing attack, fled by sea to Kiushiu. Yoshitsune promptly collected a larger fleet and followed. The Taira were overtaken at Dan-No-Ura in the Straits of Shimonoseki. The battle that ensued is one of the most famous in the annals of Japan. The Taira fleet was annihilated. The widow of Kiyomori drowned herself and the boy Emperor, her grandson, in order to disappoint the victors who wished to take them alive. The few hundred survivors who managed to escape hid themselves in the mountains of Kiushiu. There their descendants can still be moved to tears by the itinerant story-teller who recites from memory the rhythmic prose of the " Heike Monogatari," the story of their great disaster.

Yoshitsune was ill rewarded for his brilliant victories. Yoritomo seems to have feared that he might play the same game as Yoshinaka, and with better success. He commanded him, on his return, not to enter Kamakura, but to deliver up his trophies at a temple without the walls. He was obeyed, and, Yoshitsune returned to Kioto. Deprived of his command and followed by spies, he lived in constant dread of assassination. From Kioto he retired to Yoshino, and thence, with many adventures by the way, fled to his old place of refuge at Mutsu. He was, at first, well received, but his former protector died soon after his arrival ; and his son, thinking to ingratiate himself with Yoritomo, barbarously murdered his guest. Instead of the promotion which he expected, the assassin was punished for his crime by Yoritomo, who, however, is not held guiltless of complicity in it.

Legends still current among the Aino of Yezo assert that Yoshitsune made good his escape to that island ; and thence, some believe, he passed to the mainland and became famous all over Asia as the great Mongol conqueror, Genghis Khan. A number of circumstances lend some color of probability to this belief—the similarity of the names Gen and

Genghis, the correspondence of dates, the Mongol conqueror first becoming prominent a little after Yoshitsune's disappearance, and the fact that, at the height of his power, he sent an army to invade Japan. But history rejects this opinion.

The battle of Dan-No-Ura was fought in A.D. 1185. Yoritomo died of the effects of a fall from his horse in 1199. In the interval he had entirely reorganized the military and judicial administration of the Empire, and controlled all practical affairs of government from his own stronghold, Kamakura. He had obtained from the Emperor the title of shogun, with the right of transmitting it to his descendants. But scarcely was he dead when a new and unlooked-for change took place. He was succeeded as shogun by his son, Yoshiiye, under the guardianship of his grandfather, the former Taira captain, Hōjō Tokimasa. The latter kept a firm hand on the machinery created by Yoritomo, and treated his ward as the Emperors had long been treated, that is to say, he ignored him in all matters of importance. When Yoshiiye insisted on having a share in the government, Tokimasa exiled him to a monastery and there had him assassinated. His younger brother, Sanetomo, was appointed shogun in his stead, but Yoshiiye's son, a mere lad, murdered him in revenge for his father's death, and for this was himself executed.   Thus ended the main line of the Minamoto.

Hōjō and his descendants now openly took to themselves the supreme power.   Still, they did not assume the shogunate, but compelled the child Emperors at Kioto to appoint "shadow sho- guns " at Kamakura, in whose name they governed the country as regents.   In several cases, to secure still greater freedom from responsibility, the old game of resignation was resorted to, and an ex- regent, from some secure monastic retreat, directed the policy of the regent, who controlled the shogun, who was supposed to govern as representative and agent of the Emperor.

Thus the influence of the Court at Kioto was re- duced to the shadow of a shade.   The arts flourished in the new capital of the Hōjō, especially the art of metal-working connected with the fabrication of arms and armor.   The colossal Buddha of Kamakura, erected at this period, is the greatest triumph of the bronze founders' art in Japan.   The Mongol inva- sion, already referred to, was repelled, and, on the whole, the country prospered under the revived Taira despotism.   But literature fell almost wholly into the hands of the monks, who brought into use many Chinese terms, leading the way to the modern Japan- ese, which is largely composed of foreign idioms.

Sunrise Stories

Purists reject this later literature *in toto*, yet it includes some of the most characteristic products of Japanese genius. To it belong the drama, the novel, the principal histories ; and, in the period of the civil war, the lyrical drama, evolved by the monks from the old Court dances, and many curious personal narrations like that which is reviewed in the following chapter.

XIII

KAMO NO CHOMEI'S "STORY OF MY HUT"

THE troubles and disasters of the latter half of the twelfth century were nowhere more severely felt than at Kioto. The unfortunate capital was frequently the scene of sanguinary battles between the Taira and the Minamoto. The city suffered, besides, from misfortunes of its own. In 1177 a great conflagration destroyed thousands of houses and part of the imperial palace. A hurricane in 1180 was followed by the removal of the Court by Kiyomori to his fortress city of Fukuwara. Pestilence and famine ravaged the district after the usurper's death in 1181. The year of the Taira overthrow at Dan-No-Ura, 1185, was marked at the capital by a tremendous earthquake. Through most of these events Kamo no Chomei, son of a Buddhist priest of the neighborhood, was a resident in Kioto. Having lost most of his property, owing to the wars, and being disappointed in his hopes of preferment, he retired to the village of Owari, where, he complains, he was reduced to live in a cottage that could not boast of a gateway, and

151

that was scarcely a tenth as large as his ancestral
dwelling. There he appears to have stayed for ten
or a dozen years, and to have derived consolation
from that ready resource of the unpractical, the cultivation of the Muse. During this time Yoshinaka
seized Kioto, the Taira were destroyed, Yoritomo
became shogun, and died, leaving the power in the
hands of the old Hōjō Tokimasa. Chomei became
celebrated as a poet, and was invited in that capacity
to Kamakura by the shadow-shogun, Sanetomo. But
this good fortune came too late, or he soon tired of
being a witness of his patron's dissolute mode of life.
At the age of sixty he again left the world to pass
the remainder of his days in a hut that he built for
himself on the side of Toyama, or West Mountain, in
the province of Etchū. There he wrote his "Hōjōki"
—a most curious and interesting account of his life as
a hermit—in that mixture of Chinese and Japanese
abominated by latter-day critics.

In Japan it is more respectful—because less familiar—to speak of a person by the name of his dwelling than by his proper name or title. Thus the
Emperor is the "Dairi," that is, "the great gate"
of the palace; and in Tsurayuki's journal, he, the
owner, is referred to as "the Ship." The custom is
not unknown elsewhere. In similar fashion Chomei
humorously identifies himself with his hut. Later

the metaphor became a commonplace, and the word Hōjō came to be applied indifferently to a small and mean dwelling or to a Buddhist priest. The "Story of My Hut" is the story of Kamo no Chomei's life.

Thoreau speaks somewhere of the house as the man's outer garment; but to Chomei it was a second self. He dwells on the similarity of the destinies of domicile and inmate. Of the multitudinous roofs of the great city, some, indeed, last for generations, but finally fall into decay, and are torn down to make room for new buildings. Their fate is shared by the great families, their owners. More often the master and the dwelling may be compared to a drop of dew in the cup of a morning-glory flower; no one can say whether the dew will evaporate or the blossom wither first; but, in any case, what is certain is that neither will long outlast the dawn.

In his account of the memorable disasters witnessed by him (with which he points this moral) occurs a description of the great fire of April 28, 1177. It started at night in a shed used as a temporary hospital, and, a strong gale blowing from the south, swept northward in the shape of an open fan, and before morning had destroyed half the palace, the college for officials, and innumerable dwellings. Clouds of black smoke and showers of sparks veiled the more distant parts of the city, and through them the flames could be seen to leap whole blocks at a time, setting new quarters in a blaze. Thousands perished, suffocated by the smoke, crushed by falling timbers, or burned to death, and those that survived had lost all their possessions. "Foolish, indeed!" he exclaims, "the man who expects to find safety in so dangerous a place as a city."

The cyclone of February 28, 1180, affords him another example of the unstable fortunes of men and houses. Advancing hundreds of yards while one might draw a breath, it wrecked every building in its path. In some cases both walls and roof were flattened out upon the ground; in others the bare posts only were left standing. Thatch and tiles were whirled through the air like dead leaves in autumn. Meanwhile the sky was obscured with dust, and the roaring of the storm drowned the outcries of the victims, reminding him of "the wind called Go, which, on the last day, will sweep all created things before it into the abyss."

The removal of the Court in 1180, by the all-powerful Kiyomori, the famine and pestilence in the following year, and the earthquake in 1185, supply Chomei with further matter to moralize upon. Nowhere could there be secure contentment so long as one had anything to lose. To be in favor with the powerful was to live in continual fear, "like the sparrow that builds too near the eagle's eyry." On the other hand, the poor man was insulted by his wealthier neighbors, and was wretched because he could not afford to gratify the desires of his wife and family. The townsman was exposed to such dangers as he had described ; but, should he remove to the country, he suffered many privations because of the bad roads and the numerous robbers. All social relations were but further sources of injury and annoyance. The strong oppressed the weaker; the weak undermined the stronger. One's neighbor is one's enemy. To be charitable was but to surround one's self with parasites. "To pursue your own way quietly is to be treated like a madman ; but to be obliged to act exactly as others do is not to be borne." These arguments led him to the conclusion that it was best to quit the world, since he could neither reconcile himself to its ways nor change them for the better.

This was after his experience at Kamakura, where, while he and the young shogun were composing verses and laying out gardens, the crafty old Tokimasa was gathering the reins of power into his own hands. It was no place for an honest man who had eyes in his head. He fled to the mountains, and at first not feeling quite safe anywhere, wandered about in the provinces of Mino and Etchū. His hut was built of planks that hooked together, so that it might be readily taken down and moved from place to place. The floor was of earth, the roof of thatch to be obtained everywhere. Two hired carts took him, his house, and his furniture wherever he wished to go.

But when he began his book he had settled on Mount Toyama, part of the wildest mountain range in all Japan. He had been broken in health before leaving the capital of the shogun, but now " the dew of sixty years, that had been on the point of evaporating, congealed again as on a tiny blade of grass." Here, then, is an end of complaining and repining. He has no idea, he says, of composing a tract for the times, or of satirizing the vices and follies of the world. What he writes is a simple record of years passed in unaffected piety and communion with nature, while in the cities about him everything seemed relapsing into barbarism.

His hut, he tells us, was but ten feet square and seven feet high—like nothing so much as the shelter that a belated traveller might knock together for the night; but it fitted him as the cocoon fits the silk-worm. Other houses are constructed to suit everybody but their owners; family and servants, even horses and cattle, have their share in them, but his was built for him alone.

Having chosen a permanent site, he had added a few conveniences. A bamboo mat, supported from the southern side of the hut, served as an awning under which to take the air. A shelf attached to the inner wall held an image of Buddha, placed where the morning sun might strike upon its forehead. Pictures of Fugen and Fudo * hung upon the leaves of the door, and certain black boxes held his Buddhist books of devotion and some volumes of old Japanese poetry. Close by leaned against the wall a *biwa* and a *koto*; and, though he was but an indifferent performer, there was no one to criticise him, and he could at least remind himself of the pleasure he had formerly experienced in listening to the most celebrated musicians of the day. He puns upon the name of one of them. "When the wind accompanies me in the foliage of the cinnamon-trees," he says, "I can even fancy I hear the very notes of Cinnamon Dainagon." Close by his window stood his writing-table. A brazier and a wooden pillow complete the inventory of his furniture.

It is interesting to compare it with Thoreau's. The Concord hermit encumbered himself with "a bed, a table, a desk, three chairs, a looking-glass three inches in diameter, a pair of tongs, and a pair of andirons, a kettle, a skillet, and a frying-pan, a dipper, a wash-bowl, two knives and forks (*sic*), three plates, one cup, one spoon, a jug for oil, a jug for molasses, and a

* Personifications of Meditation and Wisdom.

japanned lamp." All this for the body, which to reduce to what was absolutely necessary was the object of his experiment. And, for the spiritual man, there was no Buddha with the morning sun on his forehead, no pictures nor music, nothing but books and " Nature." Nature, too, seems to have had more to say to Chomei than to the New England philosopher.

Our hermit cultivated a few herbs in a small garden, watered from a reservoir supplied by a bamboo pipe from a spring near by. The forest of Toyama furnished wild fruits and plenty of fuel. Across the shrubby valley opening on the Sea of Japan he could gaze at evening toward the home of the blessed, and see in the clouds of sunset the glories of the Western Paradise. "In Spring," he writes, "the purple wistaria blossoms wave around my hut; in summer I listen to the plaintive call of the cuckoo; in autumn the shrill voice of the cicada sounds like a dirge in my ears; in winter the heaped-up snow accumulates like the mountain of human iniquity, which melts away as quickly before the sun of virtuous endeavor."

Unlike those monks that dwelt together in communities, Chomei—no man of routine—was happy that when indisposed there was no superior to call him to account for failure to perform his devotions. He did as the spirit moved him. On the other hand,

Kamo no Chomei's "Story of My Hut"

the discipline of silence, to which he was by nature averse, was made easy to him by the absence of chattering companions. And in most other things he was out of the reach of temptation.

The warden of the mountain, living in a cottage at its foot, had a boy who sometimes accompanied the hermit at his work of gathering *kaya* blossoms (used for food), wild parsley, and wild potatoes, and in weaving straw mats which he sold to supply his other necessities. " I sixty, he sixteen," he observes, " we are often occupied with the same matters, the same thoughts."

In fine weather he would climb to the summit of the mountain, whence he could see the peaks of his native province. Or he would make a longer pilgrimage to the shrines of Iwami or to Ishiyamadera,* or to the moor of Awazu, to muse over the ruins of " old Suminari's (a former hermit's) cottage." Returning, he would stop to pluck by the way some particularly fine bunch of fern or branch of maple or of cherry, which he would take along with him to offer at some wayside shrine. By night, in lonely places among the mountains, he admired the fireflies lighting up the recesses of the woods like torches, and the monkeys crying to one another across the glen would

* A tramp overland to Iwami and back must have taken the entire summer.

bring to mind some lines from the "Myriad Leaves: "

> Bright rays of the moon
> Of shining deeds remind me,
> Of the men of old ;
> The monkeys' piteous wailing
> With sadness deep affects me.

But the morning showers, the rustling of boughs in the wind, would rouse him to more cheerful thoughts, and the cry of the pheasant, or a deer coming fearlessly to greet him, would show that degenerate humanity was far from his track.

After five years' use his hut was, at the time of his writing (March, 1212), somewhat the worse for wear. Moss covered part of the floor and dead leaves filled the hollows in the roof. From time to time he hears of the death of some man of note, and tries to guess how many of less consequence must have passed away since he came to his retreat. Palaces and hovels not a few have perished in the many conflagrations ; yet he and his hut remain. In the wilderness his lean and thinly clad figure excites no ridicule. A tunic of wistaria fibre, and a bed of leaves covered with hempen cloth, with a few kaya flowers and wild fruits suffice him. His lifelong desires are satisfied. He is free from envy, fear, and regret, and enjoys the beauties of nature, which are no man's private property.

Kamo no Chomei's "Story of My Hut"

His conclusion may serve as a specimen of Buddhist practical philosophy. All the three worlds of matter, feeling, and idea constitute one great unity which the quiet soul may apprehend and, in a way, appropriate. Of what use, in comparison, are treasures, palaces, and horses to him whose mind is not at rest? Peace has come to him nowhere but in his hut. In the city he might be made ashamed of his poverty; in the mountains he feels only pity for those who toil to so little purpose in its hot and dusty streets. "A fish never wearies of the water, nor a bird of the forest, none but themselves can tell why. Neither can he who has not experienced them judge of the pleasures of the solitary." Still, one fails of perfection so long as his heart is attached to anything of this world. To love even his poor hut and the security it affords may be wrong. "This quiet morning, having written down these reflections, I ask myself: Admitting that my aim is good—to calm my passions and to reduce to practice the principles I have always professed—yet, can I say that I have succeeded, that I am a sage or a good man, more than in appearance? Does not my conduct fall short of that of the weakest of Buddha's disciples? Of what is this the fault? Of natural incapacity, or of some remnant of worldliness not yet eradicated?" He leaves these questions unanswered and ends with a simple prayer for light.

Chomei is believed to have died in 1218, a year before the murder of his sometime patron, Sanetomo. He has been compared with Rousseau, Wordsworth, Thoreau. Their aim was indeed much the same—to secure opportunity and leisure for building up the spiritual man. The result in his case, if less striking, is more pleasing. He is free from Rousseau's moral weakness, and from Wordsworth's harsh and narrow egotism. He enjoyed nature after a more artistic, that is, a more advanced and human fashion, than Thoreau, who must have spoiled many a fine sensation in his haste to make a note of it. As to the final outcome of their philosophizing, it may be that it is not very satisfactory in any case.

XIV

THE FIGHTING MONKS AND THEIR STRANGE DIVERSIONS

In the long period of the civil wars, which were only interrupted for a time by successful Hōjō statecraft, those to whom fortune was unkind did not all, like Kamo no Chomei, flee to the mountains. There were the monasteries, which furnished, if not a safer, at least a more comfortable, retreat. Most of those who, either from choice or necessity, were out of the game of life had recourse to them. They were a refuge for the proscribed, a home for the impoverished, an asylum for deposed rulers, a place of detention for prisoners of state. All sorts of interesting people might be found within their walls—penitent thieves, and warriors sick of slaughter, delicately reared sons of noble families, and waifs of unknown parentage. The worse the anarchy in the world outside their gates, the more the monasteries grew in wealth, intelligence, discipline, and power. But their holy character did not always preserve them from assault and pillage. It was not unusual for men, who, weary of fighting, had embraced the monastic life in the hope to end their days in peace, to be obliged to take up arms again in defence of their convent. Their - fellow monks were often no whit behind these ex-soldiers in courage. In the general mêlée a warlike abbot would even sometimes take the aggressive, either to wipe off an old score or to acquire new privileges or territory. Thus, the life of a bonze was not without some spice of danger ; and, for the gentle quietist, Chomei, the hut on Toyama was, indeed, the only possible sanctuary.

The abbots and monks of the ancient foundation of Hieisan were noted above others for their militant spirit. The monastery occupied the slope of the mountain between Kioto and Lake Biwa, and over-looked the lake. It had added to its domains until they included thirteen arable valleys and the hills and forests between ; and hundreds of shrines and temples were hidden in the groves or perched boldly upon the summits. A feud of long standing existed between it and the monastery of Miidera in the low-lands near the outlet of the lake. A well-known legend relates how Benkei, the gigantic squire of Yo-shitsune, stole the big bell of Miidera and trundled it uphill to Hieisan, where the theft was looked upon as a highly meritorious action and a sufficient repara-tion for many former misdeeds. But the bell re-

The Fighting Monks

fused to give a sound when rung, and Benkei, disgusted, flung it back again.

The monks of Hieisan took a famous part in the war between the Taira and the Minamoto. Go-Shirakawa, whose accession had furnished the pretext for war, had been noted as a prince of dissolute habits, to which fact he doubtless owed the preference which the Taira chieftain, Kiyomori, accorded him. But hardly had he been placed upon the throne when he developed a surprising desire for power and capacity for intrigue; so that the wary prime-minister thought it safest to depose him and pack him off to a convent. But Go-Shirakawa was not so easily to be disposed of. As "cloistered emperor," with zealous monks for ministers and emissaries, he continued secretly to have a hand in affairs, and he is believed to have been instrumental in promoting Yoritomo's successful revolt. At any rate he welcomed his lieutenant, Yoshinaka, to Kioto, and was prompt to recognize his nominee, Go-Toba, as emperor. But when Yoshinaka undertook to usurp the supreme executive power, Go-Shirakawa marched against him at the head of several thousand sturdy bonzes. They were met by Yoshinaka's troops in the outskirts of Kioto and, though the monks laid about them valiantly with their staves, numbers and superior armament carried the day; they were routed with great slaughter, the abbot of Hieisan was taken and beheaded, and the ex-Emperor himself was put in prison. But the affair aroused intense indignation against Yoshinaka, which imperilled his position in Kioto and so contributed to the loss of the battle of Fushimi in which he was slain. Go-Shirakawa was released by the victorious Yoshitsune, and, until his death, in 1192, retained a considerable influence in politics.

The chief cause of the continued disturbances was the lack of real statesmanship among the men who by one means or another acquired control of the nation. Leader after leader fought or intrigued his way to the surface with no other idea than to keep his legitimate superiors in a position of dependence while he lived, and to transmit his titles and offices to his descendants when he died. No attempt was made to conciliate rival interests; no scope was provided for legitimate ambitions. There were but two ways to attain or to keep in place—to abuse the confidence of the lawful ruler, or to rebel against him. It was to the interest of the actual wielder of the power that the nominal head of the nation should be a child or a weak and effeminate youth, who might easily be led or, at worst, might be compelled to abdicate by a mere show of force. But the Imperial house never quite lost its hold on the loyalty of the people; and, spite of all precautions, the occupant of the throne would occasionally assert his right to govern. The emperors could not be permanently reduced to the position of merely spiritual rulers, like the high-priests of Izumi. When compelled to abdicate, their advice might yet be followed by the new incumbent, who had then to be prevailed upon to abdicate in his turn. And disaffected clans could usually find a "cloistered emperor" to sanction a rebellion, if not to incite and lead one.

In this manner Go-Toba and his successor, Tsuchimikado, had been forced into retirement by the first of the Hōjō, and were succeeded in 1211 by the Emperor Juntoku, who again proved unsubmissive, and actually "conspired" against the regent then governing in the name of the shogun, Chomei's patron, Sanetomo. The attempt failed. Go-Toba was exiled to the islands of Oki, off the western coast, where he died; Juntoku was banished to Sado, and Tsuchimikado to Shikoku. Chukyo, who succeeded Juntoku, died within a year; and the reign of Go-Horikawa, who followed him, is chiefly remarkable for a renewal of the "war" between Hieisan and Miidera.

For about a century after these events the Hōjō maintained a qualified ascendancy. Fighting was constantly going on in one portion or another of the country, but there was no general disturbance. But, at the end, the Hōjō themselves fell into the prevailing vice (for such it had become) of abdication ; and regents, shoguns, and emperors, all alike children or weaklings, were controlled by guardians or tutors, or, more often, by some irresponsible ex-regent who pulled the strings that moved all these puppets from the seclusion of some monastic retreat. The monks were, in fact, the nerves, brains, and heart of the nation, and he who would rule effectively must make use of them. But they were not won over to the Hōjō. Most of them remained stanch Imperialists.

In 1318 Go-Daigo, who had acquired the necessary reputation of being a weak and pleasure-loving prince, was raised to the throne. It turned out that he had dissembled his real character, and that he was a man of courage and ability. The Hōjō took alarm ; and, finding that he could not raise a sufficient force to hold Kioto, he retreated to the monastery of Kasagi in the romantic valley of Yoshino, not far from Nara, the ancient capital. The monks had already fortified the place. It was surrounded by mountains and appeared able to hold out until distant partisans of the Emperor might arrive to his aid. The movement was, however, premature. A Hōjō army laid siege to Kasagi. The fortifications were carried by assault and were demolished, and the Emperor was sent prisoner to Oki, with the heads of his chief advisers fixed on the sill of his palanquin, to bear him company on the way.

From his island prison, where Go-Toba had died some eighty years before, the more fortunate Go-Daigo managed to communicate with his son, Moriyoshi, who had become a priest, but was at the time in hiding in a cave in the mountains opposite Oki. Through Moriyoshi he corresponded from time to time with the most determined of his military supporters, Kusunoki Masashige, who had contrived to keep the field with a devoted band of followers, and with some among the Hōjō adherents who were disposed to come over to the Imperial cause. When all was prepared he escaped from the islands in a fishing-boat. The boat was pursued and overhauled, but his pursuers saw nothing of the Emperor. He lay in the bottom of the boat covered over from head to foot with an evil-smelling heap of dried cuttle-fish. On landing he found himself at the head of a small army, with which, taking the Hōjō generals unawares, he made a forced march on Kioto and captured the city. The troops sent against him under the command of Nitta Yoshisada and Ashikaga Takauji came over to his side. This determined many who had been wavering to take the same course and, after a short campaign, Nitta, who had been appointed to the chief command, advanced against the regent's capital, Kamakura. The town was divided into wards, each separately fortified. It was taken by assault, ward after ward, with the most desperate hand-to-hand fighting. The ex-regent Takatoki, who, though "retired," was the leading spirit of the Kamakura government, committed suicide, the town was burned, and the Hōjō domination was forever ended. But not the sorrows of Go-Daigo. War broke out afresh between the victors. The see-saw of events had brought the Minamoto again uppermost, for both Nitta and Ashikaga were of that race. But they were of very different dispositions. Ashikaga, not content with having secured the lion's share in the division of the spoils, denounced Nitta and Moriyoshi to Go-Daigo, charging them with conspiring to dethrone him. Moriyoshi was put in prison and there murdered, but Nitta succeeded in establishing the innocence of both, and was commissioned to punish Ashikaga. He was defeated, and the Emperor was again compelled to flee to Yoshino.

Ashikaga made no great effort to dislodge him. Nitta and Kusunoki, though defeated, still held out, and gave him other work to do. At length Nitta was killed in a desperate fight against overpowering odds in Echizen, and Kusunoki, after three times taking and losing Kioto, was finally routed at Hiogo, and committed hara-kiri. But the Ashikaga forces

were worn out with the struggle. Go-Daigo was allowed to die peaceably at Kasagi and to transmit the
Imperial insignia to his successors, Go-Murakami and
Go-Kameyama, who reigned like little kings of
Yvetot over monks and peasants in their happy valley, and had doubtless a much pleasanter life of it
than the new line of puppets set up at Kioto by the
Ashikaga. For half a century there were two dynasties in the land, and a desultory warfare was carried
on between the " northern emperors " at Kioto and
those of the legitimate line at Kasagi. It was ended
by the southern emperor, Go-Kameyama, abdicating
in favor of the northern emperor, Go-Komatsu ; but
this resulted in only a temporary cessation of hos-
tilities.

The Ashikaga shoguns, with few exceptions, were
even worse rulers than the Hōjō. They built
" golden " and " silver " palaces for themselves at
Kioto, while the emperors, their near neighbors,
were sunk in poverty. Go-Tsuchimikado, who died
in 1500, had to be buried by charity. The military
governors were permitted to usurp all authority in
the provinces and to establish themselves as hereditary princes. Toward the end of the period Japan
was broken up into semi-independent states, each
chief warring for his own hand, or, if it seemed
worth the trouble, setting up an opposition shogun.

Robbers infested the highways, pirates the seas and inland waters. In many parts the land lay untilled; and Kioto was several times sacked by hordes of vagabond monks, and masterless soldiers.

Yet never had the great monasteries flourished so. Never had they attained such a pitch of military power. The "fighting abbot," Takeda Shingen, conquered the two important provinces of Kai and Shinano; the bonzes had made of Osaka the strongest fortress in Japan, and the Court dared refuse no demand of the monks of Hieisan. But for their quarrels among themselves, it is impossible to say that a Buddhist theocracy might not, at least temporarily, have been established. But this was the period of the rise of the great sects, and arguments about the Way often led to hostile raids and pitched battles. Because of some doctrinal dispute Hieisan arose in all her thirteen valleys and went forth to smite Kobukuji; and ardent followers of Nichiren and of Shinran forgot the teachings of Buddha and mauled one another for the honor of their respective founders. Matters were at their worst when St. Francis Xavier and his successors came to fight fire with fire. The southern princes whom they converted needed little urging to drive the Buddhist monks of all sects from their territories. St. Francis preached in Kioto, which was falling into ruin, to a

The Fighting Monks

populace rendered dull and reckless by many disasters. But his disciples had wonderful success in Kiushiu and the nearest provinces of the main island. It is doubtful how the new religion was regarded by the first great pacificator of Japan. He certainly favored it in a material way, and even gave money to build churches, but it may have been only because he found in Christianity a valuable auxiliary in his war against the militant Buddhists.

Nobunaga was, himself, son of a village priest whom the fortunes of war had elevated to be lord of the province of Owari. By hard fighting he added the neighboring provinces of Mino, Ise, and Omi, to that domain. His control of the latter province brought him within striking distance of Kioto ; and the murder of the shogun, an incident in itself of little importance, gave him an occasion. He entered the capital, ostensibly to punish the assassins, and to secure the murdered man's brother, Ashikaga Yoshiaki, in the shogunate, but he claimed as a reward for his services the position of vice-shogun, with all the power belonging of right to the higher office. In a few years he brought the greater part of the empire under some sort of control. The princely abbots of the great monasteries were the hardest of his opponents to subdue. He lay for months before Osaka, which was defended by five large castles connected by intervallations. Three of these were captured, but still the other two held out. The monks, threatened by famine, tried to break through the besiegers' lines in a night sortie, but were driven back with terrible loss. While still held in check at Osaka, Nobunaga was threatened by the lord of Echizen and the monks of Hieisan, who made an unsuccessful descent on the garrison that he had left at Kioto. He hastened to the relief of the capital, defeated the confederates, expelled the monks, and gave the great monastery to the flames. It was revived later, but never regained a tenth part of its former importance. Osaka surrendered, and its five castles were razed to the ground.

But we are not to suppose that the monks in the day of their greatness were wholly occupied in dealing out to right and left apostolic blows and knocks. They not only found time to preach and teach, but on the dancing stages in the temple grounds a new style of entertainment was evolved from the ancient miracle plays and court dances.

Mikados in exile, cloistered emperors, regents in retreat did not follow a very ascetic mode of life. To amuse their monastic leisure a more dramatic form was given to the choric songs accompanying the old dances, then personages from ordinary life were introduced, next these alone held the stage, and the dramatic mime became the farce. The monks used these new forms of literature to convey moral and patriotic ideas.

The " Pillow of Kantamu " * is adapted from some Chinese Buddhist legend. Rosei, a native of the feudal state of Shiyoku (Chinese Shu), has passed the greater part of his life indifferent to the teachings of religion. Now he has turned pilgrim, and for many days and nights has tramped it toward the holy mountain of Yauhi, in the land of Ibara, to learn the true doctrine. At the gate of Kantamu he is met by the chorus bearing the celebrated pillow, on which whoever lays his head dreams that he has arrived at the summit of earthly felicity. He lies down to sleep while dinner is getting ready, and the vision at once begins.

A magnificently clad individual approaches. He is an ambassador from the King of Ibara, who makes known that his Majesty, moved by the consideration of the extraordinary worth of the pilgrim Rosei, has abdicated the throne in his favor. This Rosei hears, dreaming. Dreaming he mounts the jewelled palanquin and is borne to the palace, the glories of which, sung by the chorus, are otherwise left to his and the

---

* Of many attempted translations those only that are given by Mr. Chamberlain, in his " Classical Poetry of the Japanese," can be considered successful.

spectators' imagination. The chorus sings of portals wrought with jade, of crowds of gift-bearers passing through, of courtiers in silk, and armed vassals pacing the great halls within. East of the palace rises a silver hill under a golden sun, and to the west a silver moon shines down upon a mount of gold.

Rosei is now understood to have entered the wonderful palace, and, in the winking of an eye, fifty years have passed. He fears he may be growing old. But now he discovers what a treasure he has in his prime minister, who has prepared an elixir calculated to prolong his life for a millennium. Rosei drinks the potion, and, inspired by it, begins his dance.

Each round of the dance represents a thousand years; but, at the end, the happy Rosei has only to drink another cup and shake his leg again. Meanwhile, the magic vessel circulates among the guests; the poorest of his people drink long life and happiness from it; the sun and moon and stars renew their youth at its overflowing fountain; and all dance away as merrily as gnats in a sunbeam. The seasons pass so quickly, each treads on the other's heels.

CHORUS.—"'Tis Spring, for, hark ! the birds are calling."
ROSEI.—"'Tis Autumn ; see the leaves are falling."
CHORUS.—" Nay, Summer, 'tis."
ROSEI.—" Nay, 'tis not so ;
      For all the world is white with snow."

The Fighting Monks

Faster and faster move the dancers. At last Rosei forgets the cup. He wakes and finds that his age-long reign has been but

> The dream of a sinner
> While waiting for dinner.

The chorus draw the moral—life is a dream ; and Rosei, bethinking himself that this is the very heart of Buddhist doctrine, and that all the sages of the holy mountain can teach him no more, abandons his pilgrimage and returns home.

The farces that serve as interludes between the *No* or mimes deal also frequently with Buddhist themes, but from a comic point of view. The chorus is absent, and the piece usually begins with an explanatory speech by the principal actor.

The husband in the farce of " Abstraction " announces that he is in a difficulty from which he can see no way of extricating himself save by deceiving his wildly jealous " mountain spirit " of a wife. On a journey from Kioto into Mino he had made the acquaintance of a pretty girl named Hana (Flower), and the charming creature had taken so deep an interest in him that she had followed him to the capital. He had arranged to meet her that same evening, but his wife was in a devil of a temper, and, he feared, suspected something. He calls her.

HUSBAND.—"My dear, I must immediately go on pilgrimage, and not only to the temples and shrines within the walls, but also to those in the country round about, to all of them, big and little. So I will be away for a long while. I have had such bad dreams —— "

WIFE.—"Pooh! Dreams! Do not trouble about them. A slight indigestion. Or, if you must take to prayers and penance, kneel down here at home, then, and burn incense on your bare fore-arm. I have heard it is very effectual against bad dreams."

HUSBAND.—"So it may be with some persons. But to each his own physic. The penance you propose might do for a priest; but for the likes of me—a layman if ever there was one—pilgrimages have been instituted."

WIFE.—"I will not hear of it. Not out of this door do you go. Content yourself with some devotion that can be performed at home."

Thus put to it, the husband chooses what he calls "a most difficult and meritorious sort of devotion, invented of old by Saint Daruma," and which consists in covering one's self up with an "abstraction blanket" and forgetting all things, past, present, and to come. Since the merit is the greater the longer he holds out, he thinks he will require a week or two; but the wife cuts him down to a day and a night. He warns her not to come near him nor make any noise during that time, because, if she should, his efforts would be ineffectual. "No one can practise abstraction when there is a row in the kitchen."

The Fighting Monks

The wife retires ; he calls his servant. He is certain that, notwithstanding her promise, his wife will not be able to restrain her curiosity; it is therefore necessary to have somebody under the blanket. But the servant dreads his mistress's tongue so much that his master's stick has to be produced to persuade him. He is finally induced to cover himself with the blanket, and the husband joyfully hastens away to keep his engagement with Hana. Hardly is he gone when the wife peeps in "to see what it looks like." It looks very uncomfortable ; and, excusing herself on the score of her anxiety, she proffers a cup of hot tea. Taro, under the blanket, shakes his head, by way of an answer. She suggests that he at least take off the blanket for a moment, and Taro shakes his head more vigorously than before. At this she gets angry, snatches away the blanket, and discovers the servant. To save himself Taro makes a clean breast of it, and the angry wife commands him to let her take his place. By the time the change is effected the husband returns, singing and slightly intoxicated. Upon entering he sits down and gives the supposed Taro a full account of the clever sayings and doings of the pretty Hana ; how she had pressed him to drink ; how she had felt sorry for the poor little Tarokaja left at home under a nasty old blanket ; how she had blamed the heartless priests who set the temple bells a-ringing so early in the morning. Finally, having finished his story, he tells Taro to uncover himself. There is no response. He begs, he commands, he tears away the blanket—and is driven from the stage with resounding thwacks by his justly indignant spouse.

XV

THE GOLDEN CALABASHES

THE work of pacification and consolidation begun by Nobunaga was continued by his lieutenants, Hideyoshi and Ieyasu, and finished by the latter.

Hideyoshi, one of the most remarkable characters in history, was the son of a peasant of the village of Nakamura. He entered Nobunaga's service as a betto or stable - boy; but in the petty wars which that chieftain was then carrying on against his neighbors of Omi and Mino his cunning and intrepidity gained him a small command. His skill in strategy grew with the extent of the field of his operations. The soldier's water-gourd, which he had hoisted for his ensign in place of the aristocratic mon, was joined by another after every victory; and the portentous bunch of calabashes grew and grew until it might be thought a happy symbol of the union into which he was to bind the struggling principalities.

He was of diminutive stature, ugly and ill-formed, but had fine eyes, and at times a pleasant smile overcame the evil impression produced by his physical defects. His soldiers were never tired of inventing affectionate nicknames for him ; his enemies, after he had become their master, called him the " crowned monkey." He himself, having never had a family name, indulged in a profusion of aliases. The name by which he is best known was adopted in 1562. In 1591, on his retirement to private life, he took the title of Taiko, and is often referred to as Taiko Sama, or My Lord Taiko. Examples of the peasant humor which endeared him to his men are preserved in numerous anecdotes. When the superstitions of his followers proved an obstacle to his plans he was accustomed to address a confidential letter to some superior divinity, requesting him to be so good as to see that none of his subordinates were permitted to make trouble. One of these epistles, addressed to the God of Rice, is still preserved at the Todaiji, at Nara. It throws a curious light on a superstition which still exists in country places in Japan. Foxes, which are supposed to be the servants and messengers of the rice god, are believed also to have the power of bewitching people. One of Hideyoshi's servants imagined herself a subject of vulpine possession, and occasioned much trouble in the household ; and the letter asks the god to institute strict inquiries into the matter and to arrest and punish the particular fox inculpated, should it appear that he had no good reason to offer

The Golden Calabashes

for his conduct. This, no doubt, had the effect of calming the woman's fears and so expelling the demon. On another occasion, some boatmen employed to transport a number of cavalry horses across an arm of the sea demurred, saying that the sea-god, Ryugu, would be angry. Hideyoshi, instead of resorting to force, as Nobunaga would have done, had a letter indited to the "Honorable Mr. Ryugu," informing him that the men were acting in the service of the Mikado, and asking him to take measures to insure their safe passage across his domain. After having been read to the seamen, the letter was thrown into the water; and, confident that the god would not now molest them, the men performed the required service cheerfully and without compulsion.

The death of Nobunaga was the turning-point in Hideyoshi's career. The former was on his way to aid Hideyoshi in the siege of a rebel castle in Chikugo when, learning of a commotion in the palace at Kioto, he turned aside with a small escort to restore order. He lodged for the night at the monastery of Honnoji. Akéchi Mitsuhidé, one of his captains, whom he had mortified by making him the victim of some ill-timed horse-play, took this opportunity to have revenge. He, too, left the line of march with the contingent under his command, all probably his own clansmen, surrounded the Honnoji in the night, and set the buildings on fire. Seeing that escape was impossible, Nobunaga committed hara-kiri.

Hideyoshi, immediately on receiving the news, transmitted it to the chiefs who were opposing him. They might, he said, have either a temporary or a permanent peace. In any case he was obliged to raise the siege in order to punish the traitor, Akéchi; but, should they fail to come to terms with him then, he would return later with all Japan at his back. His frankness had the desired effect. The beleaguered chiefs, who would undoubtedly have fallen upon his rear had they been left to guess the reason for his re-treat, saw that they could not prevent his effecting a junction with Nobunaga's army, and that, therefore, his threat was no idle one. They accepted his over-tures, and joined his party.

Eager to reach Kioto, Hideyoshi hurried on in ad-vance of his army, and narrowly escaped being trapped like Nobunaga. Near a small Shinto temple, called Nishi-no-miya, he stumbled upon an advanced post of Akéchi's force, and in the fight was separated from his body-guard. A narrow causeway led through rice-swamps to the temple. He urged his horse along it, and, when near the enclosure, dismounted and sent the animal, mad with pain from a stab in the hindquarter, galloping back upon the enemy. Having thus gained a few moments' time, he ran into

The Golden Calabashes

the temple, where the priests were taking their daily bath. Disrobing, he plunged in among them, and his pursuers, failing to recognize him, continued their search in other quarters. Meanwhile, the main body of his guards came up, and Akéchi's men were obliged to flee.

Akéchi ruled but twelve days at Kioto. Hideyoshi's army met his on the banks of the Yodogawa and administered a crushing defeat. The traitor escaped from the field, but only to be mortally wounded by a peasant with a pitchfork. He committed hara-kiri, and his head was taken to Kioto, where it was impaled on the spot where Nobunaga had died. A number of successful campaigns against his former brothers-in-arms, who thought themselves better qualified than he to exercise the supreme command, ended in the submission of most of them. Hideyoshi was honored by the Emperor with the highest titles in his gift, and for a few years Japan was at peace under the bunch of calabashes, now wrought in gold and figured among the crests of the great families.

Recent events give uncommon interest to Hideyoshi's invasion of Korea, which he undertook in 1592, probably with the idea of keeping his troublesome subordinates employed at a distance. But his boast that he could conquer China and Korea as easily as a man could roll up an old mat and carry it

off under his arm shows little respect for the fighting
capacity of the continentals. At first the Japanese
invaders carried all before them, but dissensions
broke out between their generals, one of whom, Ko-
nishi, was a Christian, and another, Kato Kiyomasa,
a determined Christian hater. These two tried in
everything to hamper and interfere with one another,
with the result that their armies were beaten in detail by the large Chinese forces sent against them.
Hideyoshi was compelled to negotiate a peace. But
his wrath was excited by an attempt of the Chinese
to set up a sort of suzerainty over Japan by pretending to invest him with the title of king. He tore up
the precious document which would have made him
China's vassal, sent the envoys home in disgrace, and
despatched reinforcements to Korea. He died while
the success of his ambitious scheme was still doubtful,
and his brother-in-law, Tokugawa Ieyasu, recalled the
troops. The invasion of Korea had no further result
to Japan (if we disregard the continuance of peace
within her own borders) than the acquisition of numerous skilled Korean potters and other artisans,
who were induced by their conquerors to settle in
the southern provinces. The establishment of the
first kilns for porcelain and for the highly prized
faïence of Satsuma is attributed to these Koreans;
and the politic Taiko provided a market for their

The Golden Calabashes

wares, and at the same time promoted his policy of internal peace by instituting an elaborate tea-drinking ceremonial. He also encouraged his warriors to pass their leisure in writing verses; nevertheless, Hideyoshi's generals sent across from Chemulpo a junk-load of pickled ears and noses of Chinese soldiers, which were buried at a spot still called the "Ear Mound" at Kioto. Other times, other manners. Japanese armies of to-day carry civilization to China and Korea and send home no ghastly trophies of their victories.

XVI

THE PIPING TIMES OF THE TOKUGAWA

THOUGH claiming descent from a branch of the Minamoto, Ieyasu, at the outset of his career, was but the laird of the small border castle of Matsudaira. After Nobunaga's death he had at first opposed Hideyoshi, but made peace at a moment so opportune that the Taiko rewarded him with the hand of his peasant sister and the government of the Kuanto, the rich plain surrounding the bay of Yedo. When at the point of death he appointed him guardian of his young son, Hideyori, naming, at the same time, a council, with whose assistance Ieyasu was to govern the empire. His opponents in the council, charging him with disloyalty, took up arms against him, but were routed at the decisive battle of Sekigahara, in October, 1600, by which he became sole ruler of Japan. Named shogun in 1603, he captured and burned the castle of Osaka, rebuilt by Hideyoshi, in 1615, and his young ward and rival, Hideyori, is believed to have perished in the flames. Such was the origin of the great Tokugawa dynasty of shoguns

188

The Piping Times of the Tokugawa

which, profiting by work accomplished by Nobunaga and Hideyoshi, consolidated feudal Japan and ruled the country down to our own days.

The frightful state of the empire at the beginning of the Tokugawa régime is naïvely portrayed in the true tale of Granny Hikone,* as written down from memory by her grandson. Her father was a gentleman who had seen service in the wars of Hideyoshi. His holding, which would have provided a comfortable living in later and more peaceful times, owing to high prices and the frequent disturbances which prevented his reaching a market for his produce, did not suffice to keep his family from the direst poverty. The daughter grew up to womanhood with but one cotton frock to wear, which at last "did not cover her shins." After Sekigahara, their feudal lord still held out against Ieyasu. His castle was invested, and the family, with those of the other samurai, was shut up within it. The women and children were permitted to occupy the lookout tower. Cannon were by that time in use, and notice was regularly given them when the guns were about to be fired, that they might not be frightened by the noise. At first the besiegers were not supplied with artillery, but after a week or so they mounted a battery, and

*See "Mistress An's Narrative," translated by Professor Chamberlain in Transactions of the Asiatic Society of Japan, vol. viii.

one day, after the usual assurance had been given that there was nothing to fear, this battery opened fire in reply to a shot from the castle, a ball came crashing through the tower wall and killed Granny's younger brother, who was standing by her side.

The women were not without occupation, but it was seldom of a cheerful character. They cast bullets and prepared lint; and, after a sortie, the soldiers would bring them the heads they had taken to wash and prepare them for the commandant's inspection. Sometimes they would be requested to secretly blacken the teeth that the head might be taken for that of a person of distinction; for this curious custom, usually confined to married women, was practised at the time, as a piece of foppery, by the men of some of the leading families. "We were not in the least afraid of the heads," quoth Granny, "and used to sleep with a number of them on the floor and the room full of the smell of blood."

A big breach was at last made in the outer walls of the castle; it was assaulted in the night and taken, and the garrison put to the sword. But Mistress An (such was Granny's proper appellation) was spared the distressing sight. The old samurai, her father, had been Ieyasu's writing master, and his pupil held him in affectionate remembrance. The day before the assault, he was warned by a letter tied to an arrow, and was assured of safety for himself and his family, could he manage to leave the castle in time. They escaped at midnight, crossing the moat in a tub, and spent the night wandering in the rice-swamps. "Yes, indeed," would Granny say, "such were the good old times!"

The real life-work of Ieyasu began after the battle of Sekigahara, and was continued and completed by his successors, Hidetada and Iyemitsu. He took care not to make desperate enemies of those that he had conquered, leaving them some of their possessions; but he confiscated territory enough to reward his own adherents. Japan under the feudal system, as finally settled by the three first Tokugawa rulers, was divided into about nine thousand petty fiefs and two hundred and sixty greater, the rulers of which had absolute power within their own boundaries, but were obliged to pay tribute and to furnish troops to the shogun. Iyemitsu, in addition, imposed the obligation upon the feudal lords, or daimio, of residing part of each year at Yedo, where they were required to maintain residences. The governed were divided into the four classes of samurai, or gentlemen soldiers, who held lands by military service and had many privileges, farmers, artisans, including artists, and, in the lowest grade, merchants. Each lord was guaranteed aid against any other who might seek to rob him of his possessions, so long as he on his side remained in obedience to the shogun.

Strictly speaking, Ieyasu established no code of laws to govern the relations of the ruling class with the common people, but in his celebrated book of Institutes he advises his successors in the shogunate to care for the well-being of the people at large, to put down the practice of suicide, which was becoming extremely prevalent, to restrict foreign commerce, and to suppress Christianity. The right of a subject of a daimio to petition the shogun was acknowledged, but it was always dangerous to exercise it. In civil cases, a body of precedents gradually grew up and ruled judicial procedure until the adoption of the Napoleonic Code in recent years.

This may seem a crude form of government, but under it the state of the country rapidly improved. Daimios were no longer permitted to make war upon one another, and to drive even their own vassals to rebellion by harsh treatment might bring down upon them the heavy hand of the shogun. Internal commerce therefore prospered, though foreign trade was confined to the single port of Nagasaki. The lower classes grew in wealth and intelligence. The idle samurai turned, some of them, to evil courses, but the majority to study and martial exercises. The lesser arts received a degree of development seldom matched

The Piping Times of the Tokugawa

elsewhere. The government sedulously encouraged the study of the Confucian books, which taught the rule of absolute obedience to master, father, and husband; but there still were here and there, even in the Tokugawa family itself, students of the old classics of Japan, who made reverence of the almost forgotten Mikado the one rule of life.

With such matters the populace of the large cities had little concern. They were nearly all Buddhists, and they had no interest in politics. But they had, in common with those above them in station, a passionate desire for amusement, excitement, and æsthetic enjoyment, and with the advance in general prosperity they found means to gratify it. A new and popular literature grew up. The romantic drama and the novel of adventure made their appearance, and scores of clever artists devoted their talents to portraying the most noted actors in their favorite *rôles*, to illustrating the novels of Bakin, the laborious life of the common people, and every-day scenes in Yedo and along the great routes. The characteristic literature of the time is the subject of the next three chapters. In this it may be well to show the relation to that literature of those artists of the popular school who, beyond all others, have made Japan known to Western peoples.

Like the dramatists and the novelists, their contemporaries, these artists worked for the masses. Still, as to technique, the only change from the practice of the more ancient schools was toward greater refinement. In design the three distinct manners already noted continued to prevail. There were the bold effective illuminations of the Buddhist school, the brush play of the Chinese, and the minute and delicate miniature style associated more especially with the Yamato-Tosa school, but which originated also in China. But as to subjects, they were wholly taken from common life, and direct comparison with nature tended to soften and break down traditional distinctions, to fuse styles and genres and to loosen the hold of established conventions on the artistic conscience. Artists went all lengths to study their chosen subjects from nature. There are stories of a painter of moonlight scenes, Buson, who, to observe his favorite luminary more at his ease, burned a hole in the thatch of his hut, and, failing to check the fire in time, set half Kioto in a blaze; and of another, Sosen, who dwelt for a whole year with the monkeys in the forest of Osaka, adopting, so the story goes, their mode of life, the better to portray them. This character of naturalism and refined technique is common to all the art of the period. Works in metal, lacquer, porcelain, ivory, the sculpture of the friezes of Nikko, and netsukes an inch in diameter, alike

The Piping Times of the Tokugawa

share it; but it is principally evident in the paintings and books of images, the designs of which were indeed the originals that were followed by sculptors, potters, and metal - workers. That sympathy with nature which is one of the best results of Buddhist teaching in the far East took an unexpected turn in these productions. The artists of the Tokugawa time were not given to melancholy musings. The stream of life seemed to them to flow on its mysterious course merrily enough. Commonplaces about the shortness of life they answered with the assertion that life is good while it lasts. What they loved above all in nature were the manifestations of that life which appeared to them so bright, so amusing, so well worth living.

The writer of the preface to one of Hokusai's volumes of sketches tells us that all that attracted and interested that versatile artist, the features and the gestures of men, the aspects of mountains and waterfalls, of trees and flowers, each with its physiognomy, its individual expression, birds, reptiles, fishes, each living its proper life, appeared to him to show such an abundance of happiness that it rejoiced his heart. It was true all was fated to pass away, but the thought only spurred him to attempt to transmit to posterity some image of the joy which appeared to him to fill the universe.

Another preface-writer testifies to the naturalness of Hokusai's drawings.

"The young folk, who are continually tramping about," he writes, " tell me how they crossed yesterday the Fukagawa, how to-day they have been to hear the cuckoos on the heath of Asajihara, and they rattle off the names of many other pleasant places; and now they would have me rise from my seat by the window where I have been lazily spending the morning to go with them on some other excursion. Softly, my young friends! I may have a manner of voyaging of my own. Behold! I have already set out. Already I see the foliage of the trees a-tremble; the soft white clouds in the blue sky grouping themselves fantastically. I ramble here and there, aimless, without an object. Now I cross the monkey's bridge over the chasm, and listen to the echo repeat the cry of the wild stork. Now I am in the cherry-groves of Owari. Above the mists that ride on the waves of Miho I see the dark forms of the famous pine-trees of Suminoye. Again, I stand trembling on the narrow bridge of Kaneji, or hearken to the roaring of the cataract of Ono. I start. It is but a dream that I have dreamt, with this volume of Hokusai under my head for a pillow."

It is plain that the artists were on very good terms with their publishers and with the writers who fur-

The Piping Times of the Tokugawa

nished these enthusiastic prefaces, and who invented such taking titles for picture books as "The Sparrows of Yedo," "The Dust of Yedo" (a book of street-scenes), "Nature in White" (snow-scenes), and "Actors on a Holiday." Often the designer lived in his publisher's house as a member of his family, as did Utamaro, for many years of his life. Others, like Hokusai and Hiroshige, wandered about a great deal, sketching as they went. One of the former's hosts, a preface-writer, is authority for the statement that during a visit of a few days Hokusai turned out more than three hundred sketches. In return for their clever puffs and other good offices, the artists illustrated the authors of the time, and so have kept alive many a mediocre book of poems, many a pointless essay and trifle light as air. It was a time of collections and books of elegant extracts, to which the compilers gave fanciful names, such as "A Thousand Roses, Ten Thousand Violets," "The Maple Leaf Brocade of Poetry," and "Little Garret Library of Song." Authors were strictly forbidden to take their characters from real life or to refer to any public event of the day. The more serious were thrown back on the moving scenes of the civil wars, or upon the glories of the ancient Empire, the less talented or less learned turned to the lightest of light literature, to essays about nothing, "Memoirs of a Grasshopper," almanacs, guide-books, all with some pretensions to a literary style, and all profusely illustrated. But the artists were comparatively free. They might poke fun with the point of their brush at priest and daimio, hold up the mirror of art to contemporary life, both public and private, pass from the Yoshiwara to the Yashiki, from the temple to the tea-house, picture the black-hooded geisha on her way to an all-night entertainment, the nun at her prayers, the woman of the people at her daily tasks, the poetess at her writing-table. For the manners of the period one must turn, not to its literature, but to these books of sketches and albums of colored prints. Hiroshige pictures the "Fifty-three Stations of the Tokaido," the great highway between Yedo and Kioto; Hokusai, "The Hundred Views of Fujiyama;" Harunobu, the "Manners and Customs of Women;" Utamaro, the twenty-four hours of the day in the Yoshiwara; Kiyonaga, the "Festivals of Yedo;" Toyokuni, the antics of a company of actors on a holiday. Innumerable were the picture-books of plants and flowers, birds and insects, shells and fishes, landscapes, illustrations of manufactures, agriculture, and industries. Silk-worm raising and the silk manufacture, dyeing and embroidering, the manufacture of arms and armor, the raising of the staple crops of rice, tea, tobacco, millet, all furnished themes for the artist's nimble pencil.   And when at a loss for new subjects, he might turn to the processes of his own craft and illustrate, as Utamaro has done, the " Cultivation of the Picture Crop at Yedo."   Many of these impressions are among the finest examples of color-printing that the world has known, and the effect was often heightened by artistic goffering of the paper.   But the hundreds of offhand sketches, "done with one stroke of the brush," offer the most amusing, and often the most valuable, records of the time.   Hokusai's " Mangwa," in especial, enjoys a richly deserved reputation as the most astonishing collection of artistic jottings that has ever been produced.   Grotesque illustrations of the ancient legends, dreams of the smoker, fancies of enormous glow-worms descending to the earth as flashes of lightning, of monstrous eels escaping from their captors, of gigantic cuttle-fish pursuing terrified farmers, who throw down their hoes and run for their lives, alternate with comic incidents of ordinary life : the fisher whose hook catches in his attendant's hair, the burgher who takes a girdle hung out to dry on a bamboo for a ghost, the school-girl whose papers are carried away by the wind, the servant detected in stealing a toothsome morsel by her shadow being thrown upon the paper screen behind which she is hiding.   The imaginings of foolish minds are frequent sources of merriment to

Hokusai. The lazy rice-grinder, as he lifts his pestle, feels it grow heavier and heavier; surely it has stuck fast to the rice, and the rice to the mortar, and, if his wife does not exert all her strength to keep the latter down, he will never get it clear! The tea-house servant chopping up eels for dinner sees them sprout from the willow branches; the lone widower, as his tea-pot boils over, sees the pool expanded into a lake, across which sails the Ship of Good Fortune with a new bride surrounded by bales of silk and boxes of ointments, while a pair of saké jars, with cups for wings, fly on in advance to herald her coming.

Political and religious freedom were unknown, foreign commerce was prohibited, education was confined to the old Chinese-Japanese curriculum, the swords of the samurai grew rusty; but no nation ever enjoyed a more materially happy and amusing existence than did the Japanese during the two centuries and a half of the Tokugawa sway. Toward the end of the period the blessings of peace began to be followed by the curses. The country was centuries behind the rest of the world in the arts of government and of war; most of the ruling class were sunk in sloth and incapacity, and the more energetic among them secretly advocated a return to the ancient constitution of the Empire. But the arts profited

The Piping Times of the Tokugawa

to the last by the long peace, and every handicraft had become artistic. In the cities, the year was one round of festivals. Every month had its special flower-show, every trade its saint's or god's day, every temple its particular ceremony. It was a true Land of Cocaigne, watched over by its seven jolly household gods, Yebisu, the fisherman ; Daikoku, the farmer ; Benten, Bishamon, Jurojin, Hotei, and Fukurokuju.

THE DRAMA

ONCE upon a time, a pretty dancing-girl named
Okuni, belonging to the great temple at Kitsuki, fell
in love with a swaggering soldier, and ran away with
him to Kioto. The man was a sort of free lance, a
ronin, or " wave-man." * Perhaps his chief had been
slain, his clan broken up and scattered in the course
of the civil wars ; perhaps he had been dismissed his
lord's service in disgrace ; perhaps he had voluntarily
embraced a roving life, in order that those to whom
he owed fealty might not be held accountable for
some foolhardy act of his. At any rate, he was ready
with his sword. On their way to Kioto, the pair fell
in with another member of the class, who travelled
for a while in their company, until vagabond number
one grew jealous of vagabond number two, and ran
him through the body. At Kioto, from time im-
memorial, part of the gravelly bed of the river Kamo
had been reserved as a place for fairs and popu-

*The term is the literal equivalent of our " vagabond." But
a ronin was always a *ci-devant* gentleman.

202

The Drama

lar assemblies. There the couple set up a dancing platform, and Okuni gave the old sacred mirror dance for the amusement of the crowd. There is nothing to show whether she did or did not add other dances. She may possibly have appeared in some of the classic mimes, or in the part of the princess Joruri, Yoshitsune's mistress, whose romantic adventures had already been made the subject of a tragedy. Later, at Yedo, we find the pair proprietors of a regular theatre, and Okuni's swashbuckler husband become famous as an actor in the romantic drama, then first emancipated from Buddhist and classic conventions. Such, according to tradition, was the origin of the modern Japanese stage.

The species of tragedy to which Joruri has given her name—"The Pure Blue Glaze " *—is a connecting link between the mime and the modern drama. Like the No, the Joruri requires the services of a chorus which chants the story while the actors, masked and dressed in rich brocades, fall into picturesque attitudes suggested by the incidents of the narrative. We have here but a modification of the primitive religious dance with its accompanying chant. But the later drama, in which dialogue completely takes the place of narrative, arose, most likely,

* In allusion to the rare and precious old blue porcelain of China.

about the beginning of the Tokugawa period, out of the farces which served as interludes in the classical No performance.

A Japanese play is the most plastic, the least stable, literary product imaginable, if, indeed, it can be, strictly speaking, called literature at all. For only the most important speeches are committed to writing, and actors like the famous Danjūrō make more free with their text than ever did Garrick or Macready with that of Shakespeare. If there is a book of the play, it is a mere summary of the leading incidents. The subjects are usually taken from the traditions of the civil wars, and the plays themselves might be called acted histories. One set of characters succeeds another, and, as in the example to be given, there may be on the stage in the last act not a single person who figured in the first. The plot branches out in all directions, and what is to-day a minor episode, may to-morrow become the leading incident. There would, doubtless, be as many versions as companies but for the fact that a play is a family possession, transmitted from father to son like a house or an estate ; but this hardly lessens the number of changes to which it is subjected, for the owners are constantly revising and adapting it to new conditions. In short, the play as given is commonly the creation of the company which produces it, and

The Drama

which has selected from the mass of dramatic material the parts best suited to the capacity of its members. This work of selection is generally well done from a purely theatrical point of view; there is never any lack of action, and the stage setting is often superb. The impression produced on the foreign spectator if he sits out an entire performance, which frequently takes a whole day, is that he has been witnessing parts of several melodramas, pantomimes, and spectacles arbitrarily combined into some strange imperfect unity. But there is usually a leading idea or sentiment which dominates the piece from first to last, and the effect is artistically worked up from possibly tame beginnings to an overpowering climax.

The theatre is a large, rectangular wooden building. In that part of the auditory that we call the pit, divided by low partitions into family stalls, the spectators sit on cushions and, between the acts, smoke, take tea, and entertain their friends. One or more galleries run about three sides of the house. The stage, which occupies the fourth, is but little elevated, and is contrived to revolve, so that while one scene is on that which is to follow is being set, and there are no waits. Two long platforms adjoin the stage, right and left, suggesting the parodoi of the Greek theatre by the use to which they are put; for, at times, it is by them that the actors reach the stage.

Let us suppose that we have arrived early and have taken seats in one of the shallow boxes. The play is to be " The House of the Blossoming Plum Trees "— a title which leaves everything to the imagination. The actor who reads the prologue, appearing suddenly from under the striped curtain, instead of enlightening us, makes a quantity of comical blunders, and leaves us as much in the dark as ever. As he disappears, the curtain is drawn aside and reveals the stage, crowded with people dressed in antique costume. The time is surmised to be that of the Ashikaga shoguns. A tournament is in progress, and two of the retainers of my lord, Asama, are engaged in a fencing-bout, which is to be the final contest of the day. They wax warm, foul blows are dealt, and they have to be separated. Yakuro, who was the first to break the rules, insolently gives himself the airs of a victor. He is reproved by his lordship, who intimates that, had the fight been allowed to proceed, the prize would have fallen to his opponent, Hanagaki; and Yakuro retires grumbling, and vowing to be revenged for the slight put upon him.

The crowd departs; the stage revolves; it is now night in the rice-fields near a small Shintô temple. The theatre has been darkened, and in the obscurity we dimly see, staggering along the narrow pathway, a wounded man, vainly endeavoring to stanch the blood that flows from a gash in his side. His assailant follows and renews his attack. A flash of lightning enables the combatants to recognize one another. The wounded man is Issai, Master of the Ceremonies to Asama; the assassin is a former retainer of the daimio, Hoshikage, who, having been dismissed for some fault, has become a ronin, and has taken to the highway for a means of subsistence. The old man falls under repeated blows from the ruffian, who takes his purse and decamps. A light trembles in the distance in the direction opposite to that taken by the robber. It is Issai's two daughters and servant who, coming to meet him, stumble over his body in time to receive his dying injunction to pursue the assassin and exact vengeance for the murder.

Again the stage revolves; it is once more day, on the banks of a little river. There is again a great throng of people—samurai, husbandmen, artisans, peddlers—gathered to witness the distribution of the prizes won by the victors in the tournament. On the edge of the crowd some ruffians turn to annoy a poorly dressed girl; and the daimio sends two of his men, Yakuro and another, to her assistance. The crowd falls back. Hototogisu (The Cuckoo) is led forward between the two samurai, and from the long set speech which she delivers we learn her history and guess that she is to be the heroine of the play.

Sunrise Stories

When, once or twice in a lifetime, we hear, at midnight, the song of the hototogisu, sounding from the darkest recesses of the wood, we know that it is a message from beyond the grave; for the bird has its home in the trackless mountains that divide this world from the next, and never leaves them but on some ghostly errand. Such, as the heroine describes it, has been her life, as obscure and lonely, hiding in the woods by day, venturing at dusk into the villages, and wandering from place to place by night, led by a vague hope, which springs afresh after every new disappointment, to seek the kinsfolk from whom she has been separated when a child.

While she speaks, giving a long account of her wanderings, the daimio and his suite disappear; and Yakuro, who has listened attentively, and who appears to be revolving in his mind some elaborate plot, leads her after to the castle.

The first act is now over, and three distinct motives are apparent which we naturally expect to see developed in the following scenes—Yakuro's resentment, the vengeance vowed by the daughters of Issai, and the quest undertaken by Hototogisu. But the second act, as it proceeds, does not seem to advance any one of these motives.

It opens with a scene on Mount Iwata. It is winter, and the ground is covered with snow. Sev-

eral men appear, dressed like hunters, carrying between them a curiously shaped box. They set it
down to rest, and fall to chatting and laughing about
its contents and the use to which Magohei, their
leader, intends to put them. The coffer, which they
have stolen from the shrine of the mountain god,
holds the dress and mask used by the priest when he
impersonates the divinity.* It is Magohei's plan to
array himself in these and, entering Issai's house,
frighten the servants, while his band, of whom the
murderer, Hoshikage, is one, make off with the two
young girls, Ojū and Wasuragi.

One of the robbers is posted to intercept any
chance traveller, the others take up their burden and
depart. Unluckily for the worthy left on guard, a
young samurai approaches, with whom he picks a
quarrel, but who proves an expert swordsman, and
pushes his adversary, step by step, to the brink of the
precipice. At last a false move on his part and he
is over.

The stage revolves. Yukieda, the victor in the
last scene, arrives at the shrine of the mountain god
farther down the slope. The body of the robber,
fallen from the cliff, lies in his path. While he is

* Shintô has no idols, but its gods are represented in religious
dances by their priests—the oldest form, probably, of religious
ceremonial.

engaged in pushing it aside, Wasuragi, the younger of Issai's daughters, arrives to beseech the god to aid her in discovering her father's murderer. As she prays, the door of the shrine is suddenly flung open and Hoshikage and Magohei, who have been hiding there, rush upon her escort. Yukieda comes to the rescue and puts the robbers to flight; but Wasuragi, alarmed for his safety and forgetting her vow of vengeance, detains him, and they are permitted to escape. Another disaster impends over the house of Issai, and now we begin to see the true drift of the play, the real subject of which is the misfortunes of the fated family.

The third act is an example of those contrasts between the action and the scene in which Japanese playwrights are unsurpassed. It is now April; we are in the gardens of the daimio's palace; plum and cherry trees are in full bloom, and under their masses of pink and white blossoms the young wife of Asama and her mother, Yuri-no-Kata, confide to one another their jealousy and hatred of the new favorite, Hototogisu, who has stolen the daimio's affections. Yakuro appears, and the ladies pretend that they have no other concern than to admire the flowers. But Yakuro skilfully leads the conversation back to the old channel and expresses the most profound indignation at his lord's conduct in transferring his attentions from their legitimate object to a mere strolling singer of unknown extraction. For a remedy, he declares he can see none but to put the adventuress out of the way by poison. The two women eagerly seize on the suggestion. Asama is away in Kioto; the work must be accomplished before his return. The prudent Yakuro has already provided the means and leads forward a physician who has brought the poison with him. The ladies examine the phial narrowly and question him minutely about its effects. Satisfied with his answers, they reward and dismiss him. But Yakuro whispers that he cannot be depended on to keep the secret, and Yuri-no-Kata calls him back. Pretending that a service so important cannot be paid for with money only, she proposes to raise him to the rank of a samurai, and borrows Yakuro's sword for the purpose. As the doomed man, taking hold of the scabbard, bows profoundly in acknowledgment of the honor, she suddenly unsheaths the weapon and strikes his head from his shoulders.

The stage revolving shows now a yet more exquisite garden scene. In the background is the pavilion occupied by Hototogisu. In front a rivulet winds through the grounds, crossed by a rustic bridge, and pours over a ledge of rocks into a ravine. The favorite is suffering from the effects of the poison. Night falls; she dismisses her servants, who withdraw reluctantly. A bluish flame rises from the floor of the pavilion, dies away, and a ghostly something hovers in its place. It is the spirit of the slain physician, who appears to warn her and to tell her of an antidote for the poison. The phantom disappears. Hototogisu tries the remedy and, delighted with the result, prepares for sleep, shutting to the sliding screens of the pavilion.

In the meantime, from opposite sides of the garden two furies armed with naked swords advance stealthily from bush to bush. They spring upon the veranda, burst the slight fastenings of the paper walls, and, rushing upon the astonished girl, cut her down like a reed. Yuri-no-Kata enters from the rear. She had tired of waiting for the poison to take effect, and considering that steel is quicker and surer had sent the two viragos upon this errand. She congratulates them upon their success, and calmly seats herself on the mat beside her victim. Torches now light up the house, which is visible to the audience through the broken screens. The wounded woman revives and charges Yuri-no-Kata with the crime, who coldly acknowledges her share in it, orders tea and tobacco to be brought, and, sipping and smoking, looks on while the servants accomplish their task.

They are bunglers; Hototogisu only faints from loss of blood; but thinking her dead they prepare to withdraw.   Regaining a little strength, she crawls painfully from the pavilion and has reached the middle of the garden before one of them, turning, discovers her.   Yuri-no-Kata runs forward, seizes her by the hair, and dragging her across the bridge, gives the *coup de grâce ;* after which the body is thrown into the ravine.   The two young servants of the favorite, who have come upon the scene, and have watched the murder trembling, are treated likewise ; and the three beldames again make ready to depart.

But, now one of the castle watch approaches, making his rounds.   He slips in the blood, examines the traces of the murder, follows them to the ravine, and, holding out his lantern at arm's length, discovers the bodies.   He returns toward the pavilion.   Yuri-no-Kata, seeing no way of escape, and satisfied with having attained her purpose, pierces her side with the sword with which she had despatched her victim.

The fourth act passes at a tea-house in the environs of Kioto.   Asama is making a visit, *incognito,* to one of the inmates.   Hoshikage, who has become the leader of a band of thieves in the metropolis, rudely jostles him and is pushed aside.   He demands the name of the daimio, who refuses to gratify him.   Three or four other thieves spring to Hoshikage's assistance.   Swords are drawn, but the daimio disdains to unsheath his weapon.   With a few smart blows of his

fan he puts the robbers to rout, and further to show
his contempt for such cowardly assailants, he fans the
air, tainted by their presence, away from him. The
loyal Hanagaki and his servant come up. They cry
out against the daimio's folly in thus going about un-
attended, and try to dissuade him from paying the intended visit, but in vain. The party enters the tea-
house and reappears a moment after at the end of one
of the long passages already described that run along
the sides of the theatre and connect it with the
stage. At the same time there appears on the other
side the beautiful Ojū, magnificently dressed, and led
along by a servant, on whose shoulders she leans.
Elaborate compliments fly back and forth from one
balcony to the other over the heads of the spectators.
Meanwhile the scene is changed and discloses the garden of the tea-house, a pavilion lit by many-colored
lanterns at the end. A supper is laid there. The two
parties proceed to the pavilion, bow ceremoniously
to one another, and take their places, the principals
within, the attendants at a respectful distance outside
on the veranda. Everything proceeds according to
the strictest etiquette. The supper is cleared away,
and Ojū takes a koto and begins to play.

At this moment, in the darkest corner of the garden, a little flame shoots up, vanishes, and Hototogisu appears in its place. The face only is plainly

visible, the black hair floating about it is scarcely distinguishable from the background. For an instant it holds a folded letter between its lips; but the letter is dropped among the bushes, and the apparition plays on the short flute used by wandering musicians an accompaniment to Ojū's music. She is heard in the pavilion, but not seen. Ojū ceases playing in order to listen.

The apparition now tries another air, one with which Asama is familiar. He comes forward to the veranda and recognizes the vision, which he imagines to be the living Hototogisu. Amazed, he asks what can be the purpose of her visit. "To see you," she returns, "and also my elder sister. In the other world I have found the parents I was so long seeking; Issai was my father." Ojū, it now appears, had been carried off by the brigands and sold to the proprietor of the tea-house. To Asama the spirit complains of the cruel treatment she had received and vanishes; he signs to the attendants to follow; they discover only the letter in the grass, which contains a circumstantial account of the murder, and urges upon her sister the duty of taking vengeance upon Hoshikage, the first cause of all their misfortunes.

The opening scene of the next act is again at the tea-house, but seven years are supposed to have passed

away. Ojū is now well known in Kioto to be
Asama's favorite. Two new characters appear, Gorōjō, an old-time retainer of the daimio, now a ronin,
and his wife. Gorōjō is sickly, and in debt. He
has many dependants, who prey upon the little substance that remains to him. His wife no longer loves
him. She wishes to join Hoshikage, who appears with
a bag of money and offers to buy her from her husband; but Gorōjō is not yet reduced to that point
and rejects the proffered purse with indignation.
His wife laughs at him for a fool, and tells him that
she means to leave him in any case. Hoshikage departs, clinking his money, and Gorōjō follows threatening him.

The woman remains, and to her now comes Ojū,
who has overheard the altercation, and who sees an
opportunity to bring the old robber to an accounting
at last. She persuades the creature, who has a sort of
fondness for her, to tell her of Hoshikage's hiding-
place, to exchange dresses with her, and to remain
for the night at the tea-house.

The scene changes to the street. An oil-lamp is
burning at the corner, and near by is the scaffold of
a fire lookout, with shelves for buckets. Gorōjō enters, climbs up and extinguishes the light, then de-
scends again and hides behind the water-buckets. If
his wife and Hoshikage are to meet, one or the other

must pass this place, and he has determined to slay whichever is the first to arrive. Hark! He hears footsteps. It is Ojū, who comes attired in his wife's kimono. With a single blow of his sabre he takes off her head, then rips the loose, hanging sleeve from her dress, wraps the head in it, slings it over his shoulder and departs. Turning the corner he stumbles against Hoshikage; but his desire for blood is sated; the two ronin glare at one another, and each goes his way.

The last act is laid at Gorōjō's house in the least reputable quarter of old Kioto. The screens forming the front of the house have been removed so that the interior is visible; and the scene also includes part of the street without. It is noon; Gorōjō's idle and hungry hangers-on are gathered discussing the news of the murder. The body has been found, and, though the head is missing, it has been identified as that of the famous beauty, the favorite of the daimio, Asama. Gorōjō enters, stretching his limbs and yawning. He listens to the gossip at first with indifference—there is nothing to connect him with the murder—then, as Ojū's name is mentioned, with surprise, which he endeavors to conceal. Every incident connected with the murder is recounted; Ojū has disappeared; her servants have identified the body by certain marks upon it; the evidence is conclusive that she is the victim. But Gorōjō refuses to be convinced. He says not a word, but his attitude shows that he weighs each statement as with loaded scales, and regards the proof which satisfies the others as contemptible. The police have blundered, that is all. Still, he dismisses his people in order to make doubly sure by examining the head, which he has hidden away.

But his blind mother enters, and he turns back from the closet which he was about to open. The old woman offers up a prayer for his happiness and goes out. It makes him melancholy to be prayed for, and he is slow about returning to the closet. He goes to the door and closes it, and changes the position of one small article after another. Pshaw! What is this feeling that is creeping over him? He plucks up nerve, opens the door of the recess and takes out the packet. Of course! It is just as he thought! This is the sleeve of his wife's kimono. Why! how could it be otherwise? What idiots those people were who thought he had slain Ojū instead. He had a right to kill his wife, she was unfaithful; but to kill the favorite of his lord—that would be a crime little short of treason. True, he had left Asama's employ; he was a ronin. But he was still a member of the clan, and owed fealty to its head. No, no! If such a deed had been done by him, even in mistake— He removes the wrappings and recoils, stupefied ; returns once, twice, incredulous ; it is hard for him to believe, even now, that the error has really been his, and that the police were not at fault.

But at last no doubt remains ; nor does he for a moment hesitate as to what he must do. He must make reparation and die the honorable death. He sits down to write his last testament.

As he does so his wife enters brimming over with tears and with gossip about the dead Ojū. Gorōjō rises and flings her out of the house. The blind mother returns, anxious, having heard the noise of the scuffle, and she also is summarily put into the street. Then Gorōjō closes the screens and piles chests and boxes against them that he may not again be disturbed. He finishes writing, takes a small table from the recess, puts Ojū's head upon it, lights candles and places vases of flowers beside it. He draws his sword and feels its edge and point. Then, seating himself opposite the sort of altar that he has improvised, he thrusts the point of the sword into his bowels.

Meanwhile the faithless wife poignards herself in the street. Her body lies in the gutter. The blind mother, distracted, understanding nothing but that her son is in trouble, tries to force her way into the house. The barricade at last yields, but Gorōjō has already dealt himself the finishing stroke. He is not yet dead when some of his cronies return with further news to impart, and blurt it out while stupidly trying to seize the meaning of the scene before them. In their search for the murderer of Ojū the authorities have laid hands on Hoshikage, whom they have long sought to apprehend for his numerous crimes. There is no question that he will be condemned to death. Gorōjō turns on his side. "You have done well to bring the good news," he says. "It is an acceptable farewell gift."

XVIII

THE FORTY-SEVEN FREE LANCES

THAT private vengeance is not favored by heaven is evidently the moral which the exemplary author of "The House of the Blossoming Plum Trees" desired to enforce. But this was far from being a universal sentiment in old Japan ; and the most celebrated of the popular romances of the Tokugawa period has for its aim the glorification of that excessive loyalty to family and chief which too often gave rise to savage blood-feuds. "The Treasury of Loyalty" (Chiūshin-gura) relates how Yenya Takasada, a lord of Hakushiu, having been compelled to commit hara-kiri, and his fief having been confiscated as a punishment for attempting the life of an insulting court official, the karō (chief councillor) of the clan and a number of retainers took an oath to slay the enemy of their lord, whose insults had brought this fate upon them, and succeeded, in spite of the latter's watchfulness and their own weak and impoverished condition.

Yenya, with the lord of Wakasa, a baron of lesser rank, and Moronao, the court officer referred to, had been appointed by the shogun, Ashikaga Takauji, to attend upon his brother, on the occasion of the latter's visit to inaugurate a new shrine to the war-god at Tsurugaoka. Moronao was to instruct the two younger men, his coadjutors, in the etiquette proper to the occasion, but confined his instructions to Wakasa, whose councillor, Honzō, had secretly taken the precaution of bribing him. Yenya, on the contrary, he treated with contempt, and so enraged by his insults that he was with difficulty prevented by Honzō from slaying his tormentor. But merely to draw sword within the precincts of the palace was a capital offence, and though Moronao escaped with a slight wound, Yenya was condemned to disembowel himself, and his castle and estates were seized by the shogun. His retainers were compelled to seek other service or become ronin.

After Yenya had died by his own hand in the presence of his family and fighting men, the karō Kuranosuké called the latter together in the great hall of the castle and divided equally among them the contents of the treasury. There were loud cries on the part of some of the younger men for resistance to the decree of expulsion, while others, knowing how futile such resistance must be, desperately counselled self-despatch. Meanwhile, those who preferred life to either course quietly slunk away, and one Kudayū

The Forty-seven Free Lances

(of whom more hereafter), not content to follow their example, bitterly reviled Kuranosuké for his equal division of the funds, claiming that he should have received a share proportioned to his salary as one of the council. Forty-seven of the samurai remained; and Kuranosuké, seeing that the good grain had been winnowed from the chaff, made known his real plan, which was that they should deliver up the castle quietly to the shogun's commissioners, but should undergo no new obligations until such time as they might find an opportunity to compass the death of Moronao in return for that of their lord. To this all assented and signed the agreement that he had prepared with their blood. They then separated, Kuranosuké going to Yamashina, a village near Kioto, where he hired a small cottage. The wife of Yenya, Kawoyo, took up her residence in the capital.

The first task of the conspirators was to set Moronao's fears at rest and remove all suspicion of their design. That worthy, they learned, had shut himself up in his yashiki and had doubled the number of his retainers, rightly judging that the quiet submission of the clan was proof that there was a plot on foot against his life. It was certain that he would employ spies to watch them, and especially the karo, Kuranosuké. Wherefore, after the manner of other famous heroes in like circumstances, Kuranosuké began to lead a double life, squandering his money recklessly, drinking deep and often, frequenting the Yoshiwara, quarrelling with his wife and son and abusing his servants—all this openly and with the most scandalous disregard of public opinion, like a man whose principles and character had been completely unsettled by misfortune ; while, when no one was looking, he remained a model husband and father, a careful guardian of the funds intrusted to him by Yenya's wife, and above all a tireless laborer for Moronao's destruction.

The anniversary of Yenya's death came about while each party was thus engaged in watching the other's movements. Moronao had begun to find a life of constant care and suspicion prey upon his spirits and was disposed to believe, if he only dared, in the reports that reached him through his spies of Kuranosuké's dissolute habits. But Kudayū, who was now in his service, knew too well the character of his old comrade to believe in such a complete transformation. He offered to accompany a retainer of Moronao, one Bannai, to Yamashina and probe the matter to the bottom.

At Yamashina, where they had learned Kuranosuké resided, the precious pair discovered that the old karo really spent most of his time in the Yoshiwara, in Kioto, and was in very bad repute with his neighbors. Making their way to the tea-house in Gion Street which they heard was frequented by Kuranosuké, they found the latter, tipsy and blindfolded, making excellent fun for a lot of girls, the waitresses of the establishment, who were having with him a game of blind-man's buff. The two emissaries of Moronao were obliged to put up with a room on the second floor, the entire ground floor of the inn having been taken by Kuranosuké for the day.

While the two spies sipped their saké upstairs, three of the ronin approached, with a fourth man, one Heiyemon, who, though only a common soldier, wished to be allowed to enroll himself among the conspirators. Kuranosuké, rushing about blindfold in pursuit of the girls, stumbled against one of the men. "Caught! caught!" he cried. "Bring the saké; she must pay forfeit by drinking a good cup of it."

"What means this foolery, Kuranosuké?" asked the new-comer, rudely disengaging himself. "I am Yazama Jiūtaro, and here are two or three friends; we must speak with you."

"What about?" inquired the karō. "Namu! girls, the game is ended."

"We seek to know," said Yazama, after the girls had withdrawn, "when we are to set out for Kamakura?"

" Kamakura ! " echoed the karō. " That is a long way off, is it not? Wait, a scrap of verse occurs to me ; but, now I remember, it is about Yedo. Perhaps some one of you gentlemen will kindly enlighten me as to what on earth we are talking about."

The exasperated ronin were about to draw upon their chief when Heiyemon interposed to prefer his request.

" Fool ! " cried the karō. " Of what use should vengeance be to you or me? Do you not know that whether the attempt failed or succeeded our deaths must follow ? Then why be at the pains to conspire? One does not take medicine when in the hands of the executioner."

Heiyemon continued to implore his permission to join the band ; but as the karō for sole answer stretched himself upon the mats and fell asleep, the samurai withdrew, cursing their old chief.

Hours slipped by. It was near dawn when the karō's son, Rikiya, entered, awoke his father and handed him a packet. " It is from Lady Kawoyo," he said. " Moronao is about to leave Kamakura for his country seat. There it will be more difficult than ever for us to reach him. We must strike quickly or it will be too late."

" Go back to Yamashina," said the karō, " and, when night falls, send me here a covered litter."

The Forty-seven Free Lances

He was about to open Lady Kawoyo's letter when Kudayū, who had not spent much time in sleep, entered the room. Kuranosuké quickly concealed the packet in his bosom.

"Well met," he called. "It is a year, I think, since we parted, and we have each acquired some wrinkles. A good occasion this to smooth them out."

"What! Sir Kura," Kudayū returned. "Well, well! It does not answer to pick holes in a good doublet; but this is a strange way to set about your enterprise against Moronao."

"Hard words," said Kura. "I do not know of what you speak."

The two called for saké, but Kudayū, who, traitor as he was, reverenced in his way his lord's memory, superstitiously avoided taking any solid food; and was horror-stricken to see the karō devour the fish that was set before him.

"I have not heard," said he, "that Yenya has been changed into a devil-fish; nor for that matter, into a pullet, which is better eating. I will go order one."

Bannai entered while Kuranosuké was seeing about the fowl, and the two spies exchanged notes and agreed that Moronao had nothing to fear from such a heartless and conscienceless scoundrel. Their litter was in waiting. The two rogues each politely requested the other to enter first. " By your leave then," said Kudayū, and, seized by a sudden inspiration, he passed through the curtained kago and picking up a large stone that happened to be at hand he deposited it in the place that he should have occupied, then quickly disappeared under the flooring of the veranda.

" Go your way," he whispered to Bannai. " I am not yet convinced and must learn in some way the contents of the letter that Rikiya just now brought to his father."

As Kudayū had expected, Kuranosuké, seeing the kago depart, apparently heavy laden, came out to the light to read Kawoyo's letter. It was a long epistle which, as the karō unrolled it, reached the planks, and Kudayū had little difficulty in drawing part of it through one of the open joints of the floor. He read sufficient to confirm his suspicions. But he might not be believed : it was necessary to have some proof to show that the conspiracy was a fact, otherwise he might yet lose his lucrative occupation. He carefully tore away the portion of the letter that had reached his hands.

But at the same time, on the balcony above, one of Kuranosuké's playmates of the previous evening, prompted by feminine curiosity, was endeavoring by the means of her metal hand-mirror to get at the contents of the letter without being herself observed. The mirror slipped from her grasp, and Kuranosuké, looking up, recognized her. "Karu," he called, "Karu, I have taken a great fancy to you. Come down, then, and leave this place with me. See! I will pay your score and set you free from service."

The girl, though puzzled and a little afraid, was, on the whole, well pleased with the offer, and did as she was bid. Kuranosuké, rolling up the scroll, re-entered the tea-house to pay his reckoning. But Kudayū still found no chance for escape; for now Heiyemon, who was Karu's brother, came out to inquire about her bargain with Kuranosuké. Learning from her that she had read the contents of the letter, "You are a dead woman," said he. "And, worse, my chance of being received as a member of the band is lost by your fault. Why do you suppose the councillor should trouble himself about you? He means to kill you to make certain of your silence."

Karu protested that she was willing to die if her living in any way endangered the success of the plot. Upon this Kuranosuké returned, having discovered the loss of part of the scroll, and reassured them, saying that he had only intended to keep Karu out of the way until the affair was over.

"But there is a traitor here who will not get off so easily," he added. And, with Heiyemon's aid, he dragged Kudayū from his hiding-place. The unfortunate spy was gagged and bound, and, to avoid discovery, was taken and cast into the river.

Kawoyo's letter, that had caused all this coil, contained but one important item of information that had not been confided to Rikiya: Moronao, reckoning on leaving Kamakura, had dismissed most of his hired guards. It was doubly important, therefore, to strike without delay. All was ready. The arms-merchant, Gihei, of Sakai, had procured armor, weapons, and uniforms, and had two fishing-junks in readiness to take the conspirators to their destination. One thing only remained with which they were not yet provided—a plan of their enemy's residence; and that Kuranosuké obtained in an unexpected manner before the day had ended.

The daughter of Honzō, the councillor of Wakasa, who had prevented Yenya from slaying Moronao, had been betrothed to Rikiya, Kuranosuké's son, but owing to the misfortunes that had come upon the latter's family, the affair had been allowed to drop. Honzō and his daughter, however, had set their hearts upon the union; and the former, knowing that nothing would be more likely to lead to a renewal of the engagement, had been at great pains to obtain from the architect a detailed plan of Moronao's yashiki, which he intended to offer as his daughter's marriage portion. But he feared he would be ill-received if he presented himself too abruptly ; so he had his wife and daughter precede him to Yamashina to open the negotiations, while he followed disguised as a wandering musician.

In Kuranosuké's absence, his wife, Ishi, received the travellers with becoming friendliness until the subject of the marriage was broached, when she put on a cold and haughty demeanor. Though her husband and son were now ronin, she said they had not dishonored themselves by offering bribes to Moronao, and they could never forgive Honzō for having saved that monster's life. On one condition only would she listen to their request—that they bring her the head of their father and husband.

Honzō in his mendicant's garb arrived just in time to overhear this outrageous proposal. He had anticipated a refusal, but the excess of hatred manifested by Ishi made him furious. Throwing off his disguise, "Here is my head," he cried ; "take it ! Your precious husband, I hear, is become a drunkard and a madman, as well as a ronin ; and, doubtless, the son follows in the father's footsteps. My head is safe enough from their rusty swords, I'll warrant."

"You shall pay for your insolence," cried Ishi,

also beside herself; and taking a long spear from the rack, she let drive at him with all her strength. Honzō caught the weapon by the shaft and wrested it from her. Brushing his wife and daughter aside, and casting the spear to a distance, he brought Ishi to the ground and held her down. At this moment Rikiya and Kuranosuké arrived, and the former, picking up the spear and heedless of his father's orders to stay his hand, ran Honzō through the body.

Everybody now stood horror-struck at the bloody termination of the affray; while the dying man, recollecting too late the purpose for which he had come, explained that his object had been to bring about an understanding as to the marriage, had not Ishi's and his own unguarded temper led to this unfortunate result. "But all will be well if you grant me my desire," he concluded, addressing Kuranosuké. "You will now surely not let my journey have been in vain."

The karō, for an answer, pushed back the screens that hid the small garden at the rear of the cottage where, that morning, playing the mad-man, he had heaped up and fashioned two tombs of snow. The visitors understood him. The tombs were for himself and his son, whose lives would be at an end before the snow could melt. "You see," said Ishi, "that if I imposed impossible conditions it was not to insult or grieve you. Moronao must die, and my son and husband must therefore perish. Why would you speak of marriage when the bride must so soon be widowed?"

"Still, let my wishes be fulfilled," urged Honzō, feebly, "and accept from me the bridal gifts that you will find set down here in this document."

He drew the architect's scroll from his bosom and handed it to Rikiya, who exclaimed, in astonishment: "Why, this is no list, but itself the best of gifts! It is the plan of Moronao's yashiki, with gate-house and postern, barracks and private quarters, everything, even to the stores and outhouses, set down in their proper places."

"Thanks, Honzō," said Kuranosuké. "You could not have brought a better peace-offering; for this removes the final difficulty from our way."

"Let me see the plan," gasped Honzō; "you must know how to use it. The best places to gain entrance are here, and here, near the water-gate and the main gate. From these points two separate parties will have each a clear path to the great hall and Moronao's private rooms. And now let the desire of my heart be granted and the marriage proceed, though it be but for a day."

"So let it be," said Kuranosuké. "For my part, I must leave at once for Sakai, to arrange with the

merchant, Gihei, who is to furnish our arms. But
you, Rikiya, can join me to-morrow. I will make
use of Honzō's disguise." So saying, he put on the
cloak and deep-brimmed hat, and picked up the bamboo flute that Honzō had thrown aside.

But the latter was now at the point of death; his
wife and daughter were prostrate by his body; and
Kuranosuké delayed yet a moment to put up a prayer
in his behalf to Buddha. Soon the last agony was
over; the thread of life was broken; and while the
women and Rikiya began the prayers for the dead,
Kuranosuké set out upon his journey.

Gihei, who was to furnish arms and transportation
for the ronin, had been in former times the factor for
the clan, who had disposed of their produce and
bought and forwarded the goods of which they stood
in need. At the first hint of the conspiracy he had
offered his services; and his only regret was that,
being a citizen, he could not take a personal share in
the enterprise. The matter was forever in his mind,
and he spent many an hour trying to think of some
means of advancing Kuranosuké's designs; but being
a dull-witted fellow, nothing ever occurred to him
until it was suggested by the karō, who himself designed the "bat's-wing" uniforms that were to enable the ronin to recognize one another in the confusion of the attack, selected the weapons, and

arranged all the details. The only stroke of policy that commended itself to him was to send his wife, Sono, out of the way, lest some news of the expedition might leak out through her, or any harm befall her if his house were searched by the authorities.

Gihei lived and did business at the sign of the Stream of Heaven (Ama-gawa) in Sakai, the seaport of Kioto ; and in his wife's absence had for company in the house only his young son and a single serving-man. On the evening before the sailing of the expedition he was aroused about midnight by a loud knocking at his door, and, opening it, half a dozen men dressed and armed like members of the city watch rushed in upon him. Their leader placed him under arrest, and told him he was charged with complicity in the conspiracy against Moronao.

" We are acting on authority," he continued. " You will be put to the torture if you do not answer our questions truly. You had better confess at once, and tell us all that you know about the plot. It is of no use your denying your connection with it. The contents of this box, which we have seized, will suffice to confound you if you do."

The box Gihei recognized as having been shipped by him that day, full of chain-mail and weapons, on board one of the junks that were to convey Kuranosuké's men to Kamakura. "All is lost," thought he ; but determined that no information about the plans or the doings of the conspirators would be obtained from him, he broke away from his captors, and putting his knee upon the chest dared them to come on.

"Tush ! " said the leader ; "we do not suppose that anything can be got from you by killing you. But we have other means which we think will prove efficacious."

At a sign from him one of the pretended officers brought in Gihei's child, a boy about a year old ; and the spokesman of the party made as though ready to thrust the point of his sword into the child's throat. But Gihei was to all appearance unmoved.

"Come ! " cried his tormentor, "you do not mean to tell me that that chest does not contain chain armor, surcoats, spears, and matchlocks furnished by you to Kuranosuké and his fellow-conspirators ! Out with the truth or we will hack you in pieces."

"The truth is," retorted Gihei, "that I deal in arms as well as in other things. There is nothing in that for which one should be hacked in pieces. But if there is, fall to and practice the six cuts on me," and quitting the chest he made a dash upon his captors.

"Hold ! " cried Kuranosuké, throwing off the cover and springing from the chest. "No one,

The Forty-seven Free Lances

Gihei, can ask further proof of your faithfulness and constancy.'' All of his associates, some of whom had doubted Gihei might play them false, were now of the same opinion, and had lowered their weapons and were bowing, with expressions of their admiration of his courage and loyalty, to the astonished Gihei. The object of the ruse was explained, and all but three of the party returned to the junks.

At this time Sono (who had been sent back to her father without a word of explanation, and had been persecuted all day by that worthy person with orders to consider her dismissal as equivalent to a divorce and to hold herself in readiness to accept a new spouse), terrified by the prospect held out to her and anxious about her husband and child, had returned, and while Gihei was entertaining his remaining guests, had prevailed upon the servant to admit her. Gihei, hearing her voice, went out to persuade her to go back to her father's ; but as he could not tell her his actual reasons and was too dull to invent others, he did not readily succeed. He was perplexed, moreover, about the matter of the divorce, as there was no doubt that, in the circumstances, her father could compel Sono to re-marry. Sono left the house, but would go no farther than the doorstep.

The three samurai could not but hear something of the dispute, and Kuranosuké, whispering some instructions to the others, they passed out at the rear of the house and, getting around to the front as Gihei shut the door, caught the disconsolate Sono by her garments and, cutting off her long black hair, ran away with it, laughing.

Sono's outcries brought Gihei again upon the scene, and Kuranosuké and the two ronin, who had re-entered the house, followed. The difficulty was laid before them, Sono not daring to believe her eyes that the two ronin who appeared as her husband's guests were the same who had robbed her of her hair. But when Kuranosuké made a parting gift of the lost tresses to her husband and accompanied it by the advice to Sono to take temporary vows as a religious, the matter was made clear. It was, indeed, an effectual way of getting rid of unwelcome suitors.

"The separation need not be for long," said Kuranosuké, as the ronin took leave of Sono and her husband. "You will hear of us before Sono's hair has had time to grow; and I promise you that when we rush to the attack our battle-cry will be 'Amagawa.' Would that you, Gihei, were a samurai. You might then be one of us; none more brave."

The two junks with the forty-six ronin on board (for, owing to a series of unfortunate mistakes one had died by his own hand), slipped out of Sakai harbor before dawn, and in due course arrived at Kamakura.

The Forty-seven Free Lances

Moronao's house, flanked on either side by the residences of other nobles, stood on a spit of land that ran out into the bay. It could be approached both by land and by water.

The night chosen for the attempt was overcast, but the ground was white with snow. Rikiya, with half the band, was ordered to scale the wall by the front entrance. Kuranosuké, with the remainder of the ronin, were to force the water-gate, which was weaker. A signal was agreed on by which Rikiya might know that his father's men had gained an entrance.

Rikiya was the first in position. His party heard the sentry's rattle as he went his rounds within, but waited what seemed to them an age for Kuranosuké's whistle. Growing impatient, two of them climbed the wall, and let themselves drop on the inside. Before long the sentry returned, and as he passed the clump of bushes behind which they lay concealed, the two ronin sprang out upon him, and, throwing him to the ground, pinioned his arms tightly. Thus placed at their mercy the man was forced to continue his rounds led by his two captors, one of whom gave, at intervals, the customary signal with the clappers. At length, Kuranosuké's whistle from the rear told them that the water-gate had been forced, and shouting "Amagawa," they slid back the bolts of the great gate and let in the twenty men commanded by Rikiya.

The shutters of the main building were tightly closed ; but Kuranosuké had provided for that. Two of his followers carried large bundles of tall and stout bamboos strung like enormous bows, and these were now inserted between the grooved beams in which the shutters slid. When the strings were simultaneously cut, the bamboos straightening pried the beams apart, so that the shutters fell clattering in upon the veranda, and were trampled by the ronin springing to the assault. The guards and domestics, awakened by their shouts and the noise of the falling shutters, were slaughtered as they came. Bannai, who had clambered up among the rafters that supported the roof of the great hall, was descried and followed, and his dead body fell to the floor in the midst of the fleeing defenders of the yashiki.

Kuranosuké, who had seated himself on a camp stool in the garden to direct the attack, had his attention distracted for some moments by the servants and retainers of the two neighboring houses, who, aroused by the tumult, now swarmed upon the roofs with lanterns and torches, and demanded to know the cause of the uproar. He was obliged to explain to them his grievance against Moronao, and assured them that vengeance was the only object in view, that every precaution had been taken against fire, and that no damage could ensue to their dwellings. But if they thought themselves bound to come to their neighbor's assistance, he was ready for them. They replied that they were not concerned about Moronao, and withdrew.

In the few minutes taken by this parley the mêlée was over. Moronao's guards had surrendered or had been cut down, and the ronin were dispersed everywhere about the building seeking its master. But he was nowhere to be discovered, and it began to look as though he had escaped. The karō gave orders to guard the gates, and began a systematic search of the grounds and outhouses. In one of the latter, where charcoal was stored, the unlucky nobleman was found, and, his face and dress black with the coal, was dragged through the snow to Kuranosuké.

Bowing in acknowledgment of his captive's rank and briefly recounting the miseries that he had brought upon the clan, the karō politely begged him to commit hara-kiri and thus, in a manner honorable to himself and becoming his high station, to place his head at their disposal.

"You say well," Moronao replied. "My head is at your service." And, drawing his short sword, he made as if about to disembowel himself. But, instead, rising to his feet, he aimed a blow at Kuranosuké, which the latter avoided, and caught his treacherous assailant by the wrist. " A clever trick ! " he cried, " but it has not served your purpose." And, throwing his enemy to the ground : " Have at him, men," he shouted, " he is yours."

" O, happy hour ! " the ronin cried, as each buried his sword in the body of their enemy. "O, blest event ! For this have we abandoned parents, wives, and children, and lived as homeless outcasts. For this have we refused to take honorable service, that we might be free to wreak vengeance upon our destroyer. Could we live to see the udongé * bloom, never again might we hope to meet the like good fortune."

Day had dawned unnoticed. The head was now severed from the body, and after having been carefully washed, was placed upon a stand at the upper end of the hall before the mortuary tablet of Yenya, which Kuranosuké had set up there. Each ronin in turn burned incense before the tablet and called upon the soul of their dead lord to regard their act with favor. Then, forming in procession, the ronin passed out through the streets of Kamakura, already ringing with the news of their exploit, to lay the head upon Yenya's tomb and there forestall the shogun's justice by dying " the honorable death."

* A sort of wild fig which (the flowers being hidden within the fruit) is fabled to bloom only once in three thousand years.

The Forty-seven Free Lances

Such, all minor incidents omitted, is the story of the Faithful Ronin, which, in some of its many versions, was read by every Japanese brought up to the old ideas and aspirations. In one edition or another the adventures of every one of the forty-seven are recounted, and, taken together, they may almost be said to have been the Bible of feudal Japan. The tale, in its main features, is founded upon fact. The Yenya of the story was Asano, Lord of Harima, in Aki, who, having drawn sword upon one Kira Kōdsuké, a court official, was compelled to commit harakiri, as is related of Yenya, March 14, 1702. The murder of Kōdsuké (Moronao in the story) took place nine months later, at his yashiki in Yedo. With the exception of these and similar changes of name, place, and date, designed to evade the decree against the publication of events of importance to the government, the narrative follows the actual facts pretty closely. It furnishes the most striking and faithful picture of the society of the Tokugawa shogunate, with its exaggerated loyalty to family and chief to which all other sentiments were made to bow, now happily replaced by a broader and more enlightened patriotism.*

* Mr. Mitford, in his " Tales of Old Japan," gives an account of the actual occurrence. Of the different versions of the " Chiūshingura," two have been translated into English : Bakin's, the most artistic, by the late Edward Greey and S. Saito, and an earlier text by Mr. F. V. Dickens.

XIX

ADVENTURES OF A VAGABOND PRIEST

THE illustrations to one of the numerous pot-boilers thrown off by the prolific Bakin, show the author listening with an air of pleased attention to the tales told him by all manners and conditions of beings. He sits in open-mouthed admiration on his cushion embroidered with spider-webs, while Lady Benten, Buddha with his ringed staff, Hachiman with his quiver, the elemental deities of storm and thunder, and Gongen Sama,* carved in granite, recount their histories; he chuckles over a friend's "good story," good-humoredly gives a hearing to the principals in the celebrated case of Fox vs. Melon, and looks up delighted from his manuscript, while the candle burns low in the socket, to hearken to some quaint bit of gossip related by his pudding-faced servant. It is his ability to draw upon both the actual life of his own day and the legends and traditions of the past, that gives Bakin his peculiar place as the Walter Scott of Japan, and makes him the most considerable figure in

* Iyeyasu.

the popular literature of the Tokugawa times. He is at his best when his imagination moves freely in a tale of his own invention. Hence his romance, "The Stormy Moon," is one of the best examples of his genius, for, though the time of the story is thrown back to the fourteenth century, the few historical characters introduced are but slightly sketched in the background and the more important might have belonged to the Japan of his own day.

Some time after the death of Nitta Yoshisada, and during the war of the rival dynasties, * there dwelt in the mountains to the west of Lake Biwa a rough fellow who had been a soldier in Nitta's army, and who now gained a scant living by hunting. This distressed the good Buddhist, his wife, exceedingly. She often remonstrated with him, and pointed out the sinfulness of his calling, for who could tell but that human souls might be imprisoned in the wild animals that he killed? But her arguments served only to amuse him. "I will believe those priests' tales of yours," he would say, "when I become old and feeble-witted, and can no longer draw a bow or tell saké from water."

Not far from Amada's hovel a hermit had raised his grass hut on the site of an ancient temple. Where thousands had formerly worshipped there was

* See Chapter XIV.

now a vast solitude : a wild doe—no other creature—
came at the sound of the hermit's bell, and listened
to his prayers. The hunter had many times seen
her, and remarked her coat spotted with five distinct
colors, each of which betokened a magical virtue.
" What a price that hide would bring from the curio
collectors of Kioto ! " said he as often as he saw her,
and many a day he lay hid by her path, but never
got her within bow-shot. One evening, the hermit
being absent, Amada borrowed his book and bell,
and reading the services (for he was an educated
man) the doe came, as usual, to listen. The hunter
dropped the book, picked up his bow and arrows,
which he had hidden, and shot her. That night his
poor wife was taken suddenly ill ; the horror of his
deed weighed upon her ; and with her dying breath she
begged her husband to have their infant son brought up
as a priest, whose prayers might atone for both their
failings. This Amada promised, and then forgot ;
but at his death, some years later, the headman of
the nearest village, who was obliged to take charge of
the orphan, readily remembered having heard Amada
speak of it, and disembarrassed himself of the youngster at the nearest temple, belonging to his sect.

Saikei, * as he was called in religion, proved

* " Illumined from the West," that is, from India, the birth-
place of Buddhism.

clever and obedient, and became a favorite with the monks. He learned readily, and was eager to oblige. But, as he grew up, there came a time when strange desires began to trouble him. At first, he was tormented by ambition; he would fain be master of a fine temple and have many pupils to listen to his instructions; and, fearing that where his humble origin was so well known this could never come to pass, he applied to be transferred to another temple. His request was granted, and he was sent, well recommended, to Kanzaki in Settsu.

In his new situation Saikei was at first as well liked as in the old. But pride trod on the heels of ambition, and he grew intolerable to his companions. Moreover, as soon as he felt assured that he might attain the prize at which he aimed, he began to look more closely into its value, and was surprised to find how little he really cared for it. At this juncture, he began to take an interest in a young singing girl from a neighboring tea-house, who worshipped at the temple. She wore a robe of five colors, and was very pretty. It was a sin, he knew, for him to occupy himself with such matters; besides, it made him miserable; he did penance, and succeeded, after a while, in expelling the image of the pretty geisha from his mind. But every now and then the worthlessness of his life without an aim would come home to him, and, harassed by a hundred doubts, he would ask himself, in despair: "What profit is there in being a bōzu?"

One afternoon, having passed the day in study, Saikei took a stroll into the hills. It was autumn: the woods were gay with the five colors of the maples. From a rock where he had seated himself, he saw a stag and his mate start up from their lair and plunge deeper into the thicket. All nature appeared to him gracious and womanly. The sun was setting: "Oh, radiant goddess!" cried Saikei, and checked himself on the instant. In his creed the sun was ruled not by the Shintô goddess, Amaterasu, but by the Buddha of Enlightenment. Still, not only the sun but the universe in its entirety, according to the philosophers, was governed by love. Why, then, did Buddhism war against it? "If only those idle villagers had not been so bent on taking a long walk, they might have dropped me at the convent of the Shin," thought he. "Then I might be permitted to marry. But, now, my vows are taken, and I am in a net from which there is no escape."

So reasoning with himself, and paying little attention to the course that he was taking, Saikei descended the mountain. It was soon dark in the valley, and in his agitation he missed the way. The road which he took led him by the rear of the tea-house gardens of Kanzaki. A geisha was singing to a party of gentlemen in one of the small pavilions. Her voice was fresh and sweet, and Saikei, though it was late, felt compelled to stop and listen. It was only when the music ceased, and the gentlemen arose and departed, leaving presents for the singer, that he came to himself with a start, and again took what he conceived to be the nearest way for the convent. In a few minutes he was brought to a halt on the brink of a deep ravine where the road suddenly came to an end, and was obliged to retrace his steps. A little girl came out of the cottage and ran to meet him. "Mistress Lotusleaf," she said, "desires to see you. She is rich, and would give you money for the temple." "But I am not a begging priest," objected Saikei. Still he suffered himself to be led into the pavilion, which was dimly lit by a lantern screened by a branch of maple.

It was the same pretty girl he had noticed in the temple, that was seated on the mats in the little building. She had need of religious consolation, she said; but something in her manner displeased him. "Come, then, to the temple at the proper hour," he returned. "Nay," said Lotusleaf, "now, this moment, I must confess—that ever since I was sixteen I have admired and loved you." In brief, Saikei found her the most interesting of penitents. Her

contrition, when he was about to take his departure,
would move the most hardened old bōzu to stay and
comfort her; but when he consented to remain, she
laughed at her peccadilloes and his scruples. " A
little saké will not hurt you," she cried. " Come,
share this cup with me ! " And Saikei, who had
never tasted liquor before, was an easy conquest once
the wine had passed his lips.

At daybreak, the innkeeper found him fast asleep
upon the mats and, taking him for a robber, bought
from him a roll of silk that the girl had left for him
with a metal hand-mirror and a note in which she
asked him to accept these presents and expressed the
hope that they might meet again. The innkeeper,
who was not a temple-goer, praised his disguise, and
offered to buy all that he might steal while in the
vicinity. " I am no blabber," quoth he, "and do
not publish my guests' affairs. But, at present, you
seem to need another cup of the liquor you had last
night." Saikei pocketed these compliments and the
money, swallowed the saké, hid the mirror in his
bosom as a keepsake, and, to the clinking of the
rings upon his staff, which had quite a new sound for
him, took the first road that led away from Kanzaki.

It was yet early morning when he entered a little
village and seated himself in the temple yard to think
over his situation. He had broken his vows; he

could not return to his monastery. For all his shaven head and black gown he felt himself an outcast. His life was shattered like a cup upon a stone. He might profess repentance; he would be forgiven, and might in time retrieve his reputation. But the very thought of such hypocrisy sickened him; and he could not now give up the hope of again meeting Lotusleaf. He decided at last to revisit his old home.

He journeyed in a leisurely way through Yamashiro into Ōmi, but there he overheard his story gleefully related by one blind shampooer to another as he sat at breakfast, and he determined to seek a livelihood elsewhere. At Kamakura he would be far enough from all who knew him, and he might find some chance to make his fortune. The question was how to get there? His money had given out.

In this strait, he remembered having seen on the road an ox laden with salt that had licked the hand of the driver. An ingenious idea occurred to him, and revolving it in his mind, he paid his reckoning with his last coin and departed from the inn. Later in the day he met an old market woman whom he frightened by threats of hell fire into giving him as alms all the money that she had with her. It procured him a night's lodging and a bath at the next village, where he had learned the salt dealer lived. He threw a handful of salt in the hot water and dipped his clothes in it as well as his body. When they were dry, he took his way to the merchant's with an extraordinary story of how his father, who had been a wicked hunter, was now in the hell of beasts, imprisoned in the body of an ox. The poor soul had appeared to him in a dream, and he had left his distant convent to seek him ; for, surely he thought, his owner, whoever he might be, would show compassion, and would treat kindly one who had been a man and was now an ox. Ere the dealer or his wife, stupefied but nowise convinced, could interpose an objection, Saikei had drawn near the stable, where the ox, it being a holiday, was resting. The beast readily licked his salted hands, followed him into the yard, and to the amazement of the good people, proceeded to eat the priest's garments. These proofs of affection were received with every demonstration of joy by Saikei, who wept abundantly, and reminded the ox of many little incidents of his boyhood, retreating the while to save his robe, the animal eagerly following him. No scepticism could withstand this affecting scene. The miracle made a profound impression upon the old couple, who gave Saikei a good dinner, presented him with a bag of money, and permitted him to lead away the ox. At the cattle fair at Ōtsu, Saikei sold him to a wretched-looking countryman for a few dollars. His purse was now well lined, and, after a

night at the best inn, he bought a new pilgrim's out-
fit, stowed away in his knapsack some bottles of saké
and the mirror that Lotusleaf had given him, and set
forth for Kamakura, alternately praying—from habit
—and singing comic songs.

We must now turn for a little to the luckless pur-
chaser of the ox. This was one Takéakira, of Seta,
a man who had been, like Saikei's father, a soldier in
Nitta's army, and who, instead of dying with his chief
on the scarped rock in Echizen, had taken to his
heels, and had since gained a miserable subsistence for
himself, his feeble wife and two children by working as
a driver for merchants of the towns along Lake Biwa.
By extraordinary self-denial Takéakira had saved
the purchase-money for the beast that he now led
proudly home, happy in the fact that he had, at last,
six legs instead of two, and could make a start on his
own account as a carrier. Yet, greater luck, as it appeared, was in store for him. He had scarcely reached
home and received the congratulations of his family
on his purchase, when there arrived a man from
Sagami with a message from his brother, of whom he
had always believed that he had been killed in Nitta's
last battle. But Takeyasu had also made use of his
legs, and, when the country had settled down after
the wars, had obtained employment as a falconer with
a Lord Kaga, of Sagami. His lordship, on a journey to

Kioto, had obtained information of Takéakira's whereabouts and condition, and, through his brother, now
offered to take him, also, into his service. The poor
man, overjoyed at the good news, took down the two
swords, which he had carefully put away out of sight
since the day when he had disgraced himself, and
thrust them into his girdle. He was once more a
gentleman. He could not be prevailed upon to wait
until the morrow. He would part at once to thank
his brother and Lord Kaga, and make arrangements
for the moving.

Let us leave him also on his way east, and see how
his good fortune turned to evil. One day, in his
absence, an unlucky shower drove Tomosada, the salt
dealer, to take refuge in his hut. There he discovered the ill-omened ox; and concluding that he had
been deceived and that Takéakira was a party to the
fraud, he procured the assistance of the headman of
Ōtsu and his officers, and, since he could discover
neither of the culprits, had Takéakira's children arrested. He would have had the mother arrested also,
but she died as they were dragging her to the door.
The children were put to the torture, but nothing
could draw from them an admission of their father's
guilt nor make them disclose his whereabouts.

Unconscious of these consequences of his rascality
Saikei, meanwhile, continued on his way to Kamakura,

Adventures of a Vagabond Priest

by the Eastern main road, along which Takéakira was also journeying, some stages in the rear. But, well supplied with money, the former took life easily. It was winter when he reached the Hakoné Mountains, and Takéakira was then well on his way home, having arranged matters satisfactorily with his brother and Lord Kaga. One evening, Saikei found himself at nightfall in a gloomy mountain pass and far from any inn. A wood-cutter, of whom he inquired where he might find lodging, pointed out to him the way to a temple, but assured him that the place was haunted by the spirit of the late master. Saikei put on a bold countenance, and advanced, jingling the metal rings attached to his staff. It was a likely enough place for ghosts. The road led through the recesses of a pine forest and its sides were bordered with tombstones, for a great battle had been fought in the neighborhood. "I should like well enough to see a light," thought he. On the instant a flame shot up at the end of the avenue, and showed him the outlines of the temple with two crouching figures which he at once recognized for priests. Then, again, all was darkness. Our hero renewed his courage by a draught from one of his earthenware bottles, and charged blindly on the temple, bursting into the area through a postern. One of the priests had by this time lighted a lantern, and over an intervening

fence he could see into the interior. Its two occu-
pants, in the extreme of terror, were huddled close
together, and gripped each other's arms like crabs;
and, as he gazed, a momentary flame rose from behind the image of Buddha, and the two priests, with
howls of dismay, sprang to their feet and ran from
the temple.

Seized with panic, Saikei ran also. He brought
up on the bank of a little stream, and again had recourse to his bottle. It was now midnight; the
moon had come out and lit the wintry scene like
day; but the liquor had made him maudlin, and, ob-
livious of the cold and of his recent fright, he drew
Lotusleaf's mirror from his bosom, and gazed at it
long and tenderly. However, he was not yet at the
end of the night's adventures. A face appeared
suddenly upon the polished metal, that of a man,
bearded and scowling. "Thousand gods!" cried
Saikei. "Hae!" called out the new-comer. "I
will have your black robe, at least, my reverend
friend," and fell at him with a two-handed sword.

Seeing that it was only a robber, Saikei acquitted
himself manfully, warding off the fellow's blows with
his staff; then, finding an opportunity, he delivered
a swinging stroke on the animal's shins, which gave
way from under him. But, though floored, he was
not disabled, and, a second thief coming up, Saikei

was fain to try the effect of a magic formula which he had learned at the convent. To his surprise, as he repeated it, his assailants' limbs grew stiff and they stood rooted to the ground, powerless to move as a stone image.*

Reduced to helplessness, the two scoundrels were forced to confess their sins, to the amusement of Saikei, who could hardly keep from laughing at their protestations of repentance. "But, where do you live?" he demanded, as it occurred to him that even a robber's den might be a better retreat for the remainder of the night than the snowy bank of the river.

The two worthies appeared to have been stricken dumb. Each nudged the other. "Bear with us, your holiness," cried the taller of the two. "But promise to absolve us beforehand and everything shall be made known."

Saikei having granted them plenary absolution in advance, the two thieves, helping one another out, told him how, prowling about the temple while the late master was on his death-bed, they had heard him several times complain of being robbed by one of his priests of the money with which he had intended to endow the temple. Later, after the master

*Numerous instances are known of paralysis induced by fear of magic spells.

had died, the nights growing cold, they began to make use of one of the outhouses of the temple to sleep in. But the smaller of the two, Shirobaye, snored so loudly that the tall fellow, Kurobaye, fearing they might be discovered, went out to reconnoitre. The priests were awake, and much more frightened than he at Shirobaye's roarings. Finding them such cowards, they then conceived the scheme of personating the ghost of the master, and, that night, had finished by driving the priests out of their temple.

"Pardon!" cried Shirobaye. "We have sinned. But if Buddha will have mercy this time, we will never more molest a holy bōzu."

Saikei could no longer contain himself. "Ha! ha!" he laughed, "you are as green as young rice and need careful tending. Listen! I knew of your proceedings at the temple and trapped ye both because I have need of ye. Both must go to Sokokura and exchange your swords for priests' gowns, shave your heads, fast, and practise good manners. Do this for a month and then return here. Ye will find me master of the temple, and ye shall be my assistants. That will be pleasanter and more profitable than lying in wait for travellers by the river-bank these cold nights."

He gave the rascals a little money, and, for him-

self, went on to the next village, where he put up at
the best inn and spent the month in making himself
familiar with the doctrines of the Shin sect, which
enjoined on its ministers a much less rigorous discipline than that in which he had been educated.

The frightened priests had really abandoned the
temple, and he found little difficulty in having the
position of master thrust upon him, and in winning
over his congregation to the tenets he had himself
adopted. His two rogues returned, and spite of their
rude manners made passable acolytes. On the day
of his appointment Saikei laid the ghost of his pre-
decessor and recovered the stolen money, which the
absconding priests had left with a lay confederate.
This exploit established his reputation, and his fame
as a preacher and miracle-worker was extended day
by day until it attained even to Sagami.

When Takéakira had reached that town he found
his elder brother married to a young woman not altogether unknown to him or to the reader, namely
Lotusleaf. His good lord, who had been of the
party that had enjoyed her music on that evening in
Kanzaki when Saikei made her acquaintance, remembering Takeyasu's lonely condition, had sent for the
koto-player, who was happy to be so comfortably
provided for. But Takéakira had heard of her affair
with the young priest, and was by no means pleased

to have such a notorious beauty for a sister-in-law. However, he said nothing to his brother, but took an opportunity to privately threaten Lotusleaf that he would take vengeance with his own hand should he find at any time that her intimacy with Saikei was renewed.

Soon after Takéakira had left for home Lotusleaf discovered that the new priest at the neighboring temple was no other than Saikei. The woman had her scruples, and the priest his brand new reputation to maintain; but the husband was old and ailing, and might at any time make straight their way by dying. An accident hastened the desired consummation, and while Takéakira, burning for revenge on the man who had caused the destruction of his home, was on his second journey from Ōtsu, Takeyasu entered on another state of existence.

On the evening of the seventh day after the funeral, Saikei called at the house to read the prayers for the dead. The services were in progress when Takéakira returned. He had found at Ōtsu his cottage ruined, his wife dead, his children imprisoned, himself outlawed because of Saikei's crime in the affair of the ox. He had come back determined to reject the offer of Lord Kaga and to devote his life, if need be, to tracking out and punishing the priest. Entering the house, he recognized his enemy by the light of

Adventures of a Vagabond Priest

the funeral candles, and, snatching his dead brother's sword from the rack, ran in upon him. But Saikei dodged his blow and, picking up a bronze incense burner, felled him with it. He then overturned the lights and escaped. Lotusleaf entering with a tray of sweetmeats, came in Takéakira's way in the dark, and met the doom intended for Saikei. For this crime Takéakira was sentenced to disembowel himself. As for Saikei, he at once took to his heels, carrying away the temple funds, and his two accomplices returned to their old avocation.

From this point on an element of the supernatural enters into the story, and gods and spirits take part in determining Saikei's fate. Making his way back to his native Ōmi, Saikei was caught in a thunderstorm upon Kagami-yama.* A bolt fell near him splitting a huge tree and leaving a small black animal imprisoned in the cleft. He thrust his staff between the halves of the trunk and prying them apart set the creature free. It vanished in the storm. Searching himself, Saikei found that he had lost his treasured mirror, and, turning back to look for it, was soon lost, himself, in the windings of the mountain paths. The sun went down, and he was left in darkness.

After walking until he was tired, he sat down to rest at the mouth of a deep glen, and presently was

* Mirror Mountain.

aware of a light shining far ahead. Stumbling on toward it, he arrived in a few minutes at a great stone gateway, such as might be the entrance to a splendid palace; at which he wondered, for he thought he knew the position of every considerable building in those parts. The gate opened readily to his summons, and he was admitted, not to palace or monastery, but to an enormous cavern that ran far back into the heart of the mountain. The whole interior was filled with a dim white light that radiated from the garments of a lady who stood awaiting him; and beside her, wrapped in silk, lay the animal that he had set free from the thunder-stricken tree that morning.

The lady received him graciously and arranged a screen and pillow for his bed, but he could not sleep for the strangeness of the adventure and the misty light that filled the place. About midnight there came a knocking at the gate, and he heard his hostess go out to answer the summons. Apparently, the customs of the place were most primitive, yet its mistress seemed a very great lady, such as the consort of one of the early emperors might have been. Impelled by an unconquerable curiosity, Saikei arose and followed her. She stood in the dewy grass on the summit of the hill, against which rested a dense gray cloud that hid the distant landscape. For a moment, Saikei distinguished the form of a water-sprite, a

Adventures of a Vagabond Priest

messenger from the sea-god; and he heard these words : "It is your stint. To-morrow, rain must pour from Obata to Musa."

Plainly his hostess was a rain-goddess; for the deities, he knew, were ordered much like earthly daimios, who were bound to render service in rotation to the shogun. The lady turning beheld Saikei, and seeming not in the least offended, said, smilingly : "Listeners must join in the plot. Now, promise that, in addition to what you have already done for me, you will take my husband's place to-morrow. That is he on the mats, within. You freed him from the cleft tree ; but his arm is broken, and he cannot carry out the sea-god's instructions. You will ride the clouds in his place and take care that the rain falls where it is needed ? "

"I am not a holy hermit," muttered Saikei. "I cannot perform such wonders."

But the lady, still smiling, promised to instruct him. "It is nothing," said she. "You have only to maintain your balance, direct the cloud by your will, and shake the bamboo sprinkler with discretion. And I will teach you other magic means of controlling springs, and streams, and every form of water. But you must promise to use your knowledge for good ends."

Saikei promised, telling himself that magical power

might somehow restore to him Lotusleaf and secure
him against Takéakira, little dreaming that both
were dead.

The following day he guided the clouds and dis-
tributed the rain over the growing rice fields. But
as he grew accustomed to the position the business
seemed a dull one ; therefore he raised the sprinkler
aloft and shook it vigorously. Immediately lightning
issued from beneath him, the thunder-drums rattled,
and a furious storm of wind and rain broke over Ōmi.

Saikei turned his attention to the dwelling of his
old friend, the salt dealer, stripped off its roof, and
sent the lightning dancing about his premises. But in
the midst of his sport he slipped from the cloud and
fell heavily into the ruined stable. There he was
caught by one of the servants, and, while insensible
from his fall, was bound hand and foot. Next day,
he was bundled into a hamper and taken to the
castle.

When brought before his judges, Saikei recovered
his senses and bethought him of the lessons in magic
that he had received from the Lady of Kagami-Yama.
He threw off the cords that bound him, and, rising in
air, passed from the view of his accusers uninjured by
the arrows, javelins, and other missiles shot or hurled
after him. Drawing a cloud about him, he willed
himself carried in the direction of Mount Iwato, and

looking down, he perceived, cowering over a little fire of leaves and brushwood, where they were heating some saké, his two companions in roguery, Shirobaye and Kurobaye, whose ragged garments and sunken cheeks showed that the world had gone badly with them since their palmy days in Sagami. At his desire the cloud deposited him near them unperceived. He was the subject of their talk.

"A very hard nut to crack, indeed," said Kurobaye. "Yet Madame Lotusleaf's brother-in-law was too much for him. Hae! It rejoices me to know that such a man could be made to feel the effects of fear, and be taught to run like another."

"Well, he has no more to fear from that hungry Takéakira," replied the giant. "What a blessing," he continued, "to be born a samurai, to be permitted to rip one's belly open and save one's honor when caught in a little felony, instead of dying a dog's death by the headsman or on the cross, as will you and I."

"True," answered his companion. "But, if the old fellow be dead, his son and daughter are expert with their weapons, the boy with bow and arrow, the girl with spear and poniard. Let the master look out."

"I do not fear them," said Saikei. It was however his dread of a blood feud that now determined him to retire to the spot where, when he was a child, had stood the hermit's grass hut. The place was difficult of access; and he posted his two assistants on the only pathway by which it might be approached, with orders to allow no one to come near him. It was his intention, by means of the spells taught him by the rain-goddess, to dry up the springs and cut off the water-supply of the province until the governor and his protégées should come to terms and guarantee him immunity for the past. He would then abjure magic, seek out and marry Lotusleaf, and live thereafter as a respectable layman. But the gods withdraw their favor from those who do evil that good may come of it. The children of his enemy were informed by a vision where to find him. Taye, disguised as Lotusleaf, ascended to his retreat, led by the tinkling of his bell through the fog with which he had encompassed the mountain. The robbers, believing her the koto-player's ghost, retreated before her, and Saikei, also deceived, allowed her to approach him; again, as at Kanzaki, he lost his self-control, and with it, his magic power; and he was beheaded by her brother who, with a party of armed men, had followed.

From a note appended by the author we learn the curious scheme of retributive justice that underlies his plot. That the sacrilegious hunter might not

Adventures of a Vagabond Priest

benefit by his son's prayers, the latter was permitted to be seduced from virtue by Lotusleaf, who was no other than the deer of five colors that Amada had slain. Takêakira and Takeyasu were punished not only for their desertion of their chief, but because it was their father's impious curiosity that had led to the hunter's crime. Thus evil produces evil until its gathering clouds are dispelled by some act of devotion like that of the children of Takêakira.

Elsewhere Bakin hesitates before the mysteries of fate and free will; but retails from old books much curious information about healing plants, about arrows of mugwort of magical virtues, thunder animals, cocks that swallow live coals and rats that live in fire; but, he adds, there is nothing to show that such tales are true, at present. His views on such matters would be commended by the Society for Psychical Research. "Strange happenings should be investigated, and should not be made light of because they are not easy to understand," he writes, and he gives as the result of his investigations into the nature of thunder, that it is caused by vapors of saltpetre and sulphur which uniting, explode like gunpowder ignited by the heat of the sun. But however much at fault Bakin's natural philosophy may be, his characters are real and human, and since his day Japan has seen no writer of fiction to equal him.

XX

CONCLUSION

WITH Bakin we may close our survey of the imaginative literature of Japan. The present generation and the last have been busy making history and laying foundations of fact for future novelists and poets to build upon and have had no time for artistic creation. But before drawing any general conclusions from the past, before attempting to characterize in a few words the national genius that has expressed itself in the dramatic dances and quaint legends of the "age of the gods," in the Buddhist stories of saints and hermits, the courtly poetry of Nara and Kioto, the narratives of the civil wars, and the popular plays and novels of the Tokugawa period, it is necessary to pass quickly in review the momentous changes which have made the present the most striking and the most glorious reign in the annals of Japan. If the past throws light upon the present, much more does the present illumine the past, and it were as unwise to give a picture drawn exclusively from the literature of the past as it is to look upon the progressive Japan of to-day

Conclusion

as wholly a product of modern external conditions.
For this reason the outlines at least of the history of
the revolution must be given, in order that the more
recent events, which are in everybody's memory, and
which have raised Japan to the position of a first-rate
power and to be the foremost agent of modern civilization in the far East, may be seen in their true relations with the historic background.

Few Japanese who have had a share in the revolution have written about the extraordinary scenes
through which they have passed; but the story of
these scenes has often been told from a European or
American standpoint by authors, sometimes preju-
diced, but more frequently ignorant of the most
important forces at work. To a young Japanese regarding the movement from the inside and sharing in
the ideas and aspirations involved in it, it naturally
presented quite another aspect from that shown in the
pages of these writers. In its later stages the movement has been represented as a sudden and irrational
surrender to ideas entirely foreign to the national
character, as a movement which must end in national
self-effacement. It is now abundantly evident that it
never had any such tendency, but was from the start
impelled and guided by a lofty and far-seeing patriotism. History is full of such apparently sudden
changes; but it is found that they were always pre-

ceded by long periods of silent preparation. So was it with Japan, where the movement toward a new order of things may be said to have begun with the Tokugawa *régime* itself.

The Japan that Bakin knew and drew so well, feudal Japan in kimono and hakama, two-sworded, Chinese-lettered, with its wealth of art and legend and its happy ignorance, protected from the outer world, as by a thick and thorny hedge, by the Tokugawa policy of non-intercourse, lives still in the memories of many who witnessed all the changes that culminated in the great revolution in 1868. Brought up in a southern castle town (Saga in Hizen), the present writer,* remembers well the mediæval customs then in force. Each day, awakened by the noise of a universal clapping of hands—the entire population of the city greeting the morning sun—he has risen to an early breakfast of tea and salt prunes, intended more as a sort of sacrament to purify the soul than as food to nourish the body. After the daily hot bath and worship at the household shrine of Buddha came a more substantial meal of bean soup, boiled rice, and pickled radishes; and then the walk to school through the fields and gardens of the walled samurai quarter, a belt of cultivated ground and scattered dwellings drawn close about the castle, and itself enclosed on all

* T. Takayanagi.

Conclusion

sides by the multitudinous roofs of the city. Each house stood in its own rice-fields and vegetable-gardens, irrigated by channels drawn from the river, which here came out to the light after a subterranean course through the lower town. The stream circled through the castle moat, gay in summer with the huge pink blossoms of the lotus, and passed out again in darkness, running under crowded streets and close-packed houses. The citizens were required to show their wooden pass-tickets at the gates before they were permitted to enter the castle precincts.

At school we were taught to read and write Chinese as well as Japanese ; and on cold winter nights, in a big annex to the school building, we practised fencing with bamboo swords and wooden spears, and also wrestling in the Japanese manner, calculated to give strength and suppleness to every portion of the body. In summer we had games of polo, and were taught to shoot with bow and arrow from horseback. In fact we were trained as though we were still in the Middle Ages.

On summer holidays the limits of our excursions were Kitayama (North Mountain) on the north, and Kawakami (River Head) and the harbor town of Hayatsuyé, or Morodomi, some three miles to the east, where Prince Nabeshima kept a man-of-war. But oftener we spent the day in fishing for eels or clamming, up to the thighs in the black mud of the river flats at low tide. Returning at night, the farmers' drums and gongs resounding from far and near and their countless lanterns swaying at the end of long bamboo poles as they paced about their fields would make the whole country-side seem at times as though it were held by an armed force ; but the only warfare that was waged was against the iné mushi, the rice insect, which, if not thus disturbed and frightened, would devour the growing crop. Nothing could really be more peaceful or more antiquated than were all our surroundings.

Yet, at this time, the revolutionary sentiment was coming to a head and soon there was to be real clashing of arms, and marching and countermarching, and bloody battles.

The restrictions imposed by the Tokugawa upon foreign commerce and the discussion of current events had had among other results that of turning a large share of the mental activity of the time into antiquarian channels. The literature of the ancient empire was studied and annotated. Scholars like Motoöri contrasted the simplicity of the Shintô rites with the corruptions that had crept into later Buddhist practice, and the unity and strength of the ancient imperial organization with the divisions and the weakness of the feudal system. Thus the edicts in-

Conclusion

tended to prevent the very possibility of a public opinion adverse to the government had exactly the opposite effect, and there grew slowly up during the seventeenth and eighteenth centuries a party which, while making no overt sign of opposition, exerted a powerful pressure in favor of the court at Kioto and correspondingly weakened the authority of the Yedo government. Strangely enough, the head and front of this movement had been the Prince of Mito, the head of one of the three great Tokugawa families entitled to share in the succession to the shogunate. In the beautiful garden of his castle, now the public park of the town, the stone bench is shown where, on the bank of a small ornamental pond, the antiquarian prince was in the habit of receiving and chatting with the scholars that he had gathered about him to aid in the compilation of his great work, the "Dai Nihongi," a huge collection of biographies, still the chief book of reference for the history of the ancient empire and the Middle Ages.

His son and successor saw further reason for disliking the dual system of government in the failure of the authorities at Yedo to resist the foreign demand that the country be thrown open to commerce. In a memorial to the shogun he pointed out that the general policy of the European powers in Asiatic countries was first to obtain concessions as traders and then to foment disorder and conquer the country piecemeal. He reminded the government of England's opium war against China, of the disadvantages under which the Japanese would have to enter into competition with other nations, and of the danger of disappointing the samurai, who were convinced that if there must be a war with the foreigners, it had better begin at once. And he followed up his memorial by confiscating the bells of the Buddhist temples in his province and casting them into cannon. In fact, both Kioto and Yedo were crowded with samurai, some of whom had accompanied their lords, who offered their services to repel the threatened invasion, while others had left their homes singly or in small groups, and had journeyed to one or the other capital for the same purpose.

Some of these last, belonging to the Mito clan, soon found work cut out for them that was much to their mind.

The leading man in the shogun's government was Ii Kamon no Kami, Daimio of Hikoné. He had become convinced of the danger of longer withstanding the demands of England, France, and the United States, and set about putting down the opposition to his policy with a high hand. He banished Mito from the capital and made him prisoner in his own castle. For this he was set upon by eighteen ronin

Conclusion

of the clan, as he was going from his own residence in Yedo to the shogun's palace, on the morning of March 23, 1860. His guard was overpowered, he was dragged from his palanquin and despatched, and the head was taken to Mito, where it was displayed on a pike over the castle gate. This was followed by attacks on the foreign embassies by other ronin, by the murder of the bully Richardson * by a Satsuma man, the attempt of the Prince of Chōshū to close the Straits of Shimonoseki, and by the bombardment of that place by English, Dutch, French, and American men-of-war, and of Satsuma's capital, Kagoshima, by the English. The destruction of Kagoshima, a city of 180,000 souls, took place in August; that of Chōshū's batteries and ships at Shimonoseki in September, 1863.

These actions made it more than ever apparent that Japan in its feudal condition could not cope with nor secure justice from the western powers. But the clans that had suffered were by no means cowed. In the south, owing to the proximity of the Dutch settlement at Nagasaki (the only open port under the

---

* Richardson was an English merchant of Shanghai who, visiting Japan on his way to England, insulted the Daimio of Satsuma by forcing his way through the latter's guard, one of whom cut him down. He had been warned by his companions that the act would be regarded as an outrage, but, in a spirit of bravado, spurred his horse into the ranks of the procession.

feudal *régime*), were many who had got a glimpse of the great world beyond the Tokugawa hedge. Long before the arrival of Commodore Perry or the bombardment of Shimonoseki, it had been known there that Japan was far behind Europe and America in the sciences, and in the art of war. The result of the bombardments, therefore, was that the southern and western clans came to a common understanding to effect the overthrow of the shogunate and the restoration of the empire; they bought new ships and cannon, hired foreign military instructors and sent abroad parties of picked students to report on the reforms necessary to enable Japan to hold her own against the rest of the world. It was at this time that the writer, then twelve years old, was sent from Saga to the school maintained by Prince Nabeshima at Nagasaki, to be instructed in English.

Rev. Dr. G. F. Verbeck, the first American missionary in Japan, was the teacher, and it may fairly be said that he had remarkable success, considering that he was obliged to teach English through the medium of Dutch, there being then no English-Japanese dictionary or grammar in existence. We had also French military instructors, and it was our chief delight to visit at houses in the foreign settlement that were opened to us, and the foreign men of war in the bay. To the old dislike of foreign things

Conclusion

and foreign ways, which had been very strong even at the south, had succeeded by this time a great enthusiasm, because we desired (but without rancor) to be able to thrash the foreigners, if necessary, in our turn.

Suddenly the older boys were called north, and next we heard of battles at Kioto and at Osaka, in which the troops of the southern coalition, though outnumbered almost ten to one, had beaten those of the shogun's party. It was demonstrated that Japanese soldiers could profit by discipline and modern weapons.

The fight was now no longer against the treaties, which had received the imperial sanction : it was to unify the country under the Emperor Mutsuhito, who had just succeeded to the throne. The shogun, Iyemochi, had died, and had been succeeded by the son of the old Prince of Mito, Tokugawa Yoshinobu. Imbued as the latter was with the traditions of his race, the leaders of the imperial party had had little difficulty in inducing him to resign all his powers into the hands of the new emperor. But his partisans, who by this act were themselves deprived of place and power, had precipitated a conflict. They had attempted to enter Kioto with ten thousand men, but had been repulsed by a force of fifteen hundred gathered from the Satsuma, Choshiū, Tosa, Hizen, and other imperialist clans. The capture of Osaka and Yedo and the deposition of the last of the shoguns followed, and the emperor entered Yedo, henceforth known as Tokio, in November, 1869.

By that time I was a student in the university (then called Kaiseijo) at Tokio, and witnessed the entrance of the Mikado, the last great function in the ancient manner, with daimios in black lacquered palanquins, samurai marching afoot, and runners at the head of each division of the procession tossing from hand to hand long bamboo poles tipped with globular masses of black or white paper ribbons. There were still after that many fluctuations of popular sentiment, which did not come over all at once to the new order of things ; and twice we students were compelled, to avoid provoking unpleasant remarks, to resume the historic samurai dress, hakama, two swords, and top-knot. But in the same year came the abolition of the daimioates, the last and crowning act of the revolution. Feudal Japan was no more.

Nothing can be farther from the truth than the notion that the revolution was the *consequence* of the foreign ministers' demands. Their action undoubtedly had the effect, wholly unlooked for by them, of precipitating a crisis which was sure to occur in any case. The country required to be more closely

Conclusion

united, more systematically organized, and even if it had remained cut off from the rest of the world the feudal organization was doomed. Nor should the anxiety of the Japanese to conform to modern ways be put down to a sudden epidemic of imitativeness. It was due to the desire of self-preservation. The national existence was felt to depend on Japan being enabled to take her place among the most progressive people of the earth. Here, indeed, a desire to forestall compulsion was active; but not in the restoration of the empire, which was an absolutely spontaneous act, and was carried out against the desires of the European ministers, who had become accustomed to obtain from the shogun's government whatever they wanted, and were, of course, desirous that it should be confirmed in power.

One who knows something of the early history of the country can in a measure account for the revolution and for the startling progress subsequently made. The Japanese first appear in history as a proselytizing and conquering people, spreading by force of arms and diplomacy their nascent civilization and anthropomorphic creed among the fetish-worshipping barbarians of the main island. Later we find them welcoming the mild teachings of Buddha, and incorporating them with their own belief, and with renewed zeal pushing the frontiers of their empire northward. The main cause of the long and desolating civil wars was the lack of an apparent outlet for the energies of the fighting class, and of an ideal higher than fealty to clan and chief. And now that Japan is once more provided with a mission, and is called upon to lead in the civilization of the far East, we see revived the eagerness to learn and to teach, the unanimous determination to advance, that marked the palmy days of the ancient empire.

There is another marked characteristic to be noted —a tendency to go lightly laden and to throw off and reject whatever is found to be unassimilable. In Japanese literature and art this trait is more marked than any other. There is much in both that has been unquestionably borrowed from the Chinese, but it has been sublimated and spiritualized, has been freed of Chinese sensuousness and of Chinese didacticism.

In more practical matters we have seen how the militant sects, both Christian and Buddhist, were put down when it became plain that they but tended to add to the turmoil from which the country was suffering; and in our own days the feudal edifice of Iyeyasu, become a hindrance, has been completely swept away. But the military skill and endurance acquired during centuries of warfare, the altruistic spirit and the love of nature fostered by Buddhism,

Conclusion

remain, along with the original endowment of the race, its courage, loyalty, its love of light and purity, its belief in its high mission.

A readiness to take the higher way and to show it to others, and a proneness to relieve the springs of action, thought, and feeling of all unnecessary weight, are the leading characteristics of the Japanese, as shown both in their literature and in their history. It is not without reason that Japan has adopted the morning sun, the source of light and standard of purity, for the emblem upon her banners. It is not quite the fact that "Japanese civilization is based upon altruism," as a recent traveller, Mr. Henry T. Finck, has put it; but it comes perhaps as near to that ideal condition as is possible in this imperfect world.